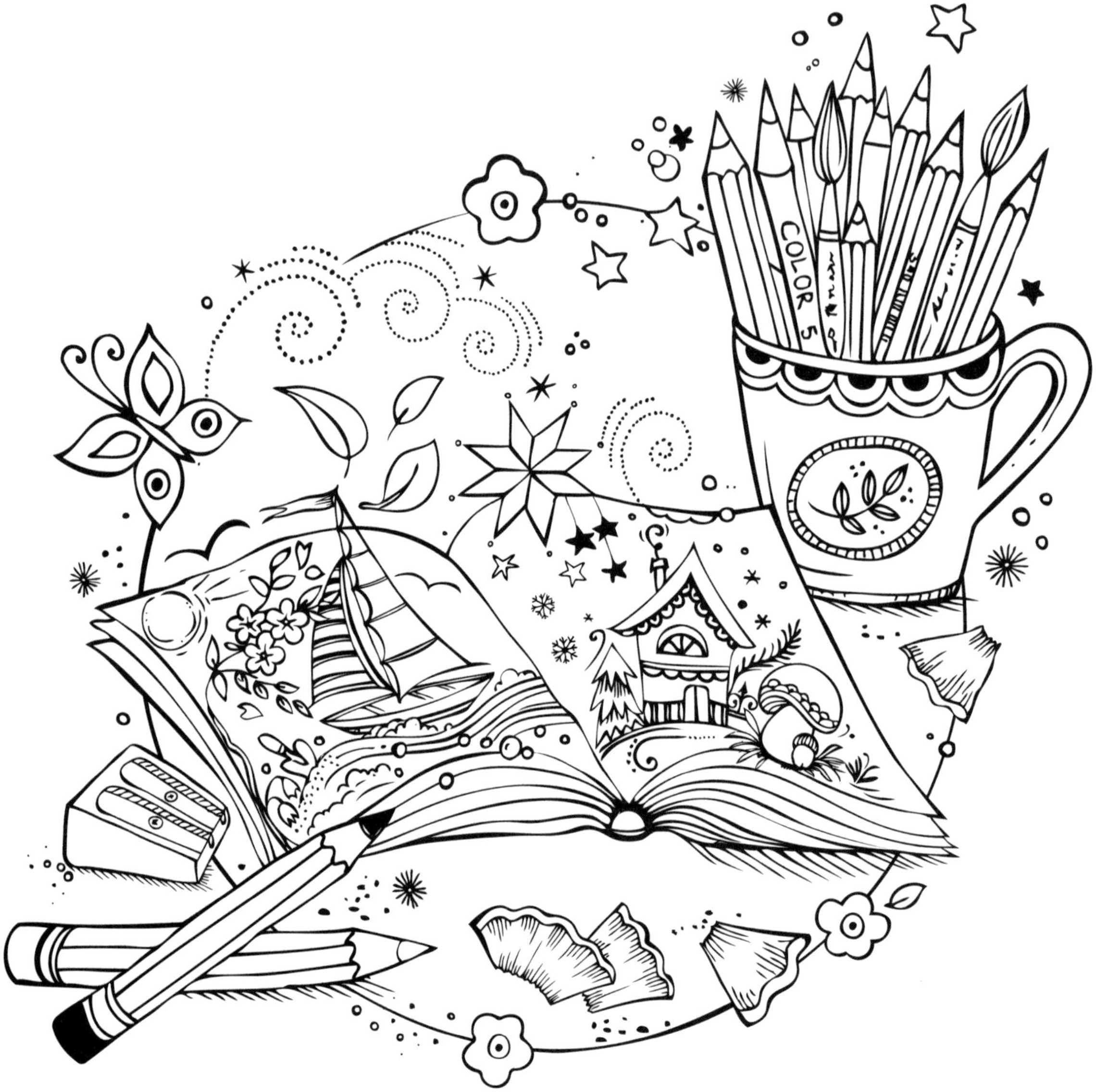
COLOR 5

Rita Berman
HIDDEN
Seasons
Coloring Book

Walter Foster

Quarto.com
WalterFoster.com

© 2025 Quarto Publishing Group USA Inc.

Published in 2025 by Walter Foster Publishing, an imprint of The Quarto Group, 100 Cummings Center, Suite 265-D, Beverly, MA 01915, USA.
T (978) 282-9590 F (978) 283-2742

Original Edition first published in Germany
Mein Spaziergang durch die Jahreszeiten
© 2018 by Bastei Lübbe AG, Köln
Cover design and illustrations: Rita Berman
Editing: Mareike Neukam
Layout: Judith Knabe
Production: Appel & Klinger, Schneckenlohe
ISBN: 978-3-404-60991-8
Find us on the internet at luebbe.de
See also: lesejury.de

All rights reserved. No part of this book may be reproduced in any form without written permission of the copyright owners. All images in this book have been reproduced with the knowledge and prior consent of the artists concerned, and no responsibility is accepted by producer, publisher, or printer for any infringement of copyright or otherwise, arising from the contents of this publication. Every effort has been made to ensure that credits accurately comply with information supplied. We apologize for any inaccuracies that may have occurred and will resolve inaccurate or missing information in a subsequent reprinting of the book.

Walter Foster Publishing titles are also available at discount for retail, wholesale, promotional, and bulk purchase. For details, contact the Special Sales Manager by email at specialsales@quarto.com or by mail at The Quarto Group, Attn: Special Sales Manager, 100 Cummings Center, Suite 265-D, Beverly, MA 01915, USA.

29 28 27 26 25   1 2 3 4 5

ISBN: 978-0-7603-9611-7

Cover design and illustrations: Rita Berman
Translation: Catherine Venner

Printed in China

I've spent 365 days mindfully watching the cycle of the seasons and am now convinced that each season possesses its very own magic. Here is a collection of my favorite drawings. I hope that you will be as enchanted as I am by the changes in nature.

Have lots of fun coloring in this book.
Rita Berman

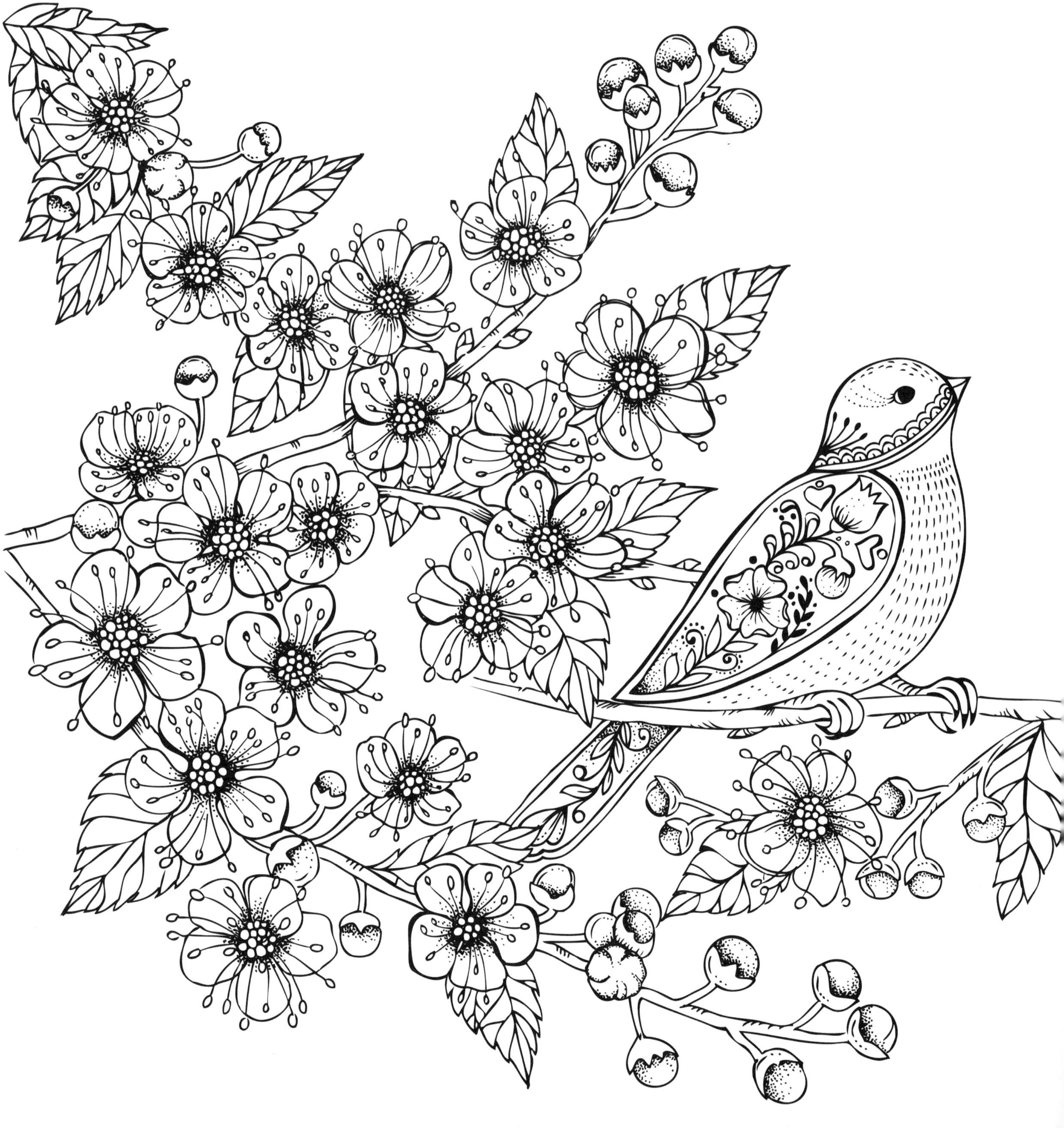

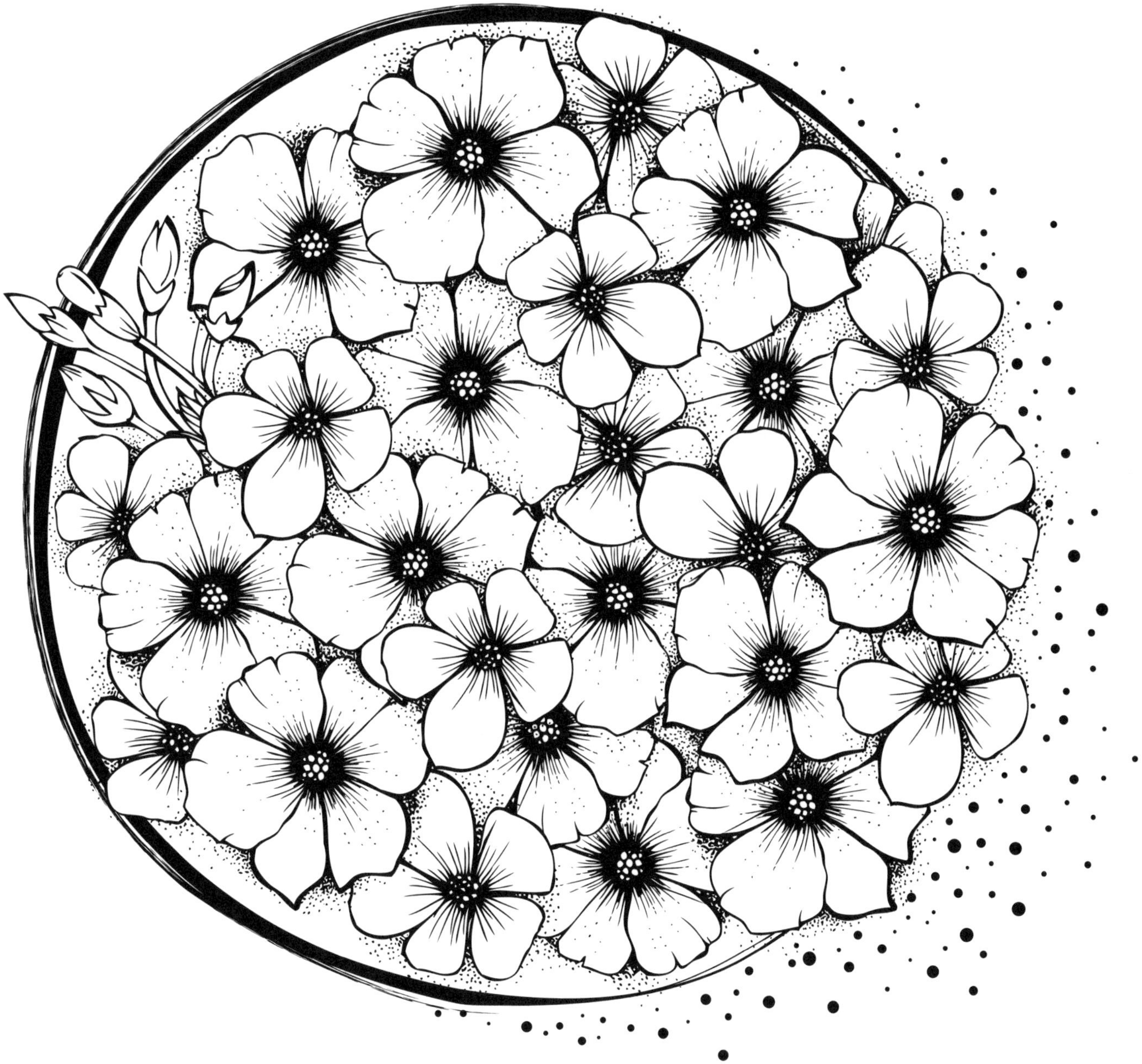

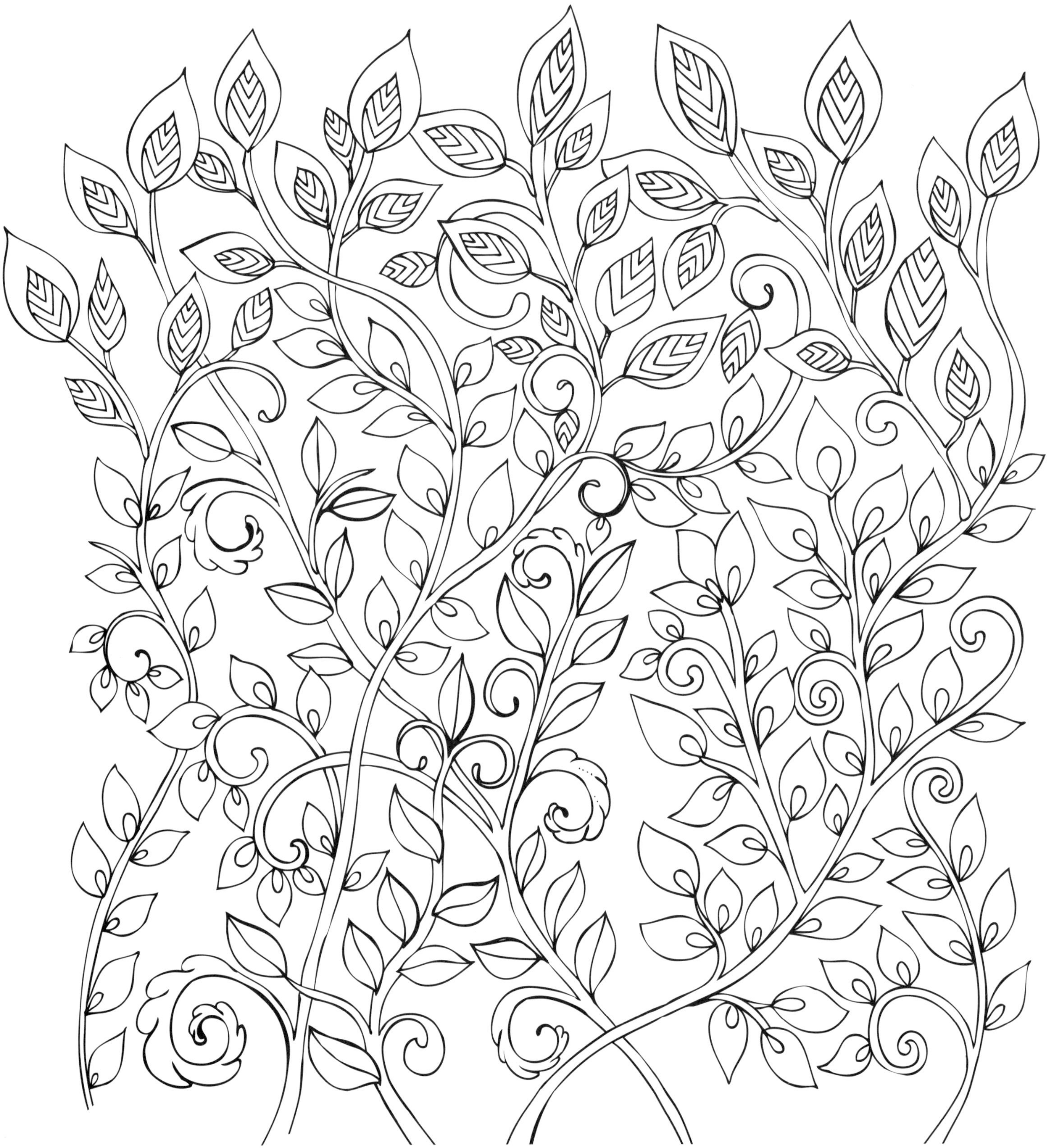

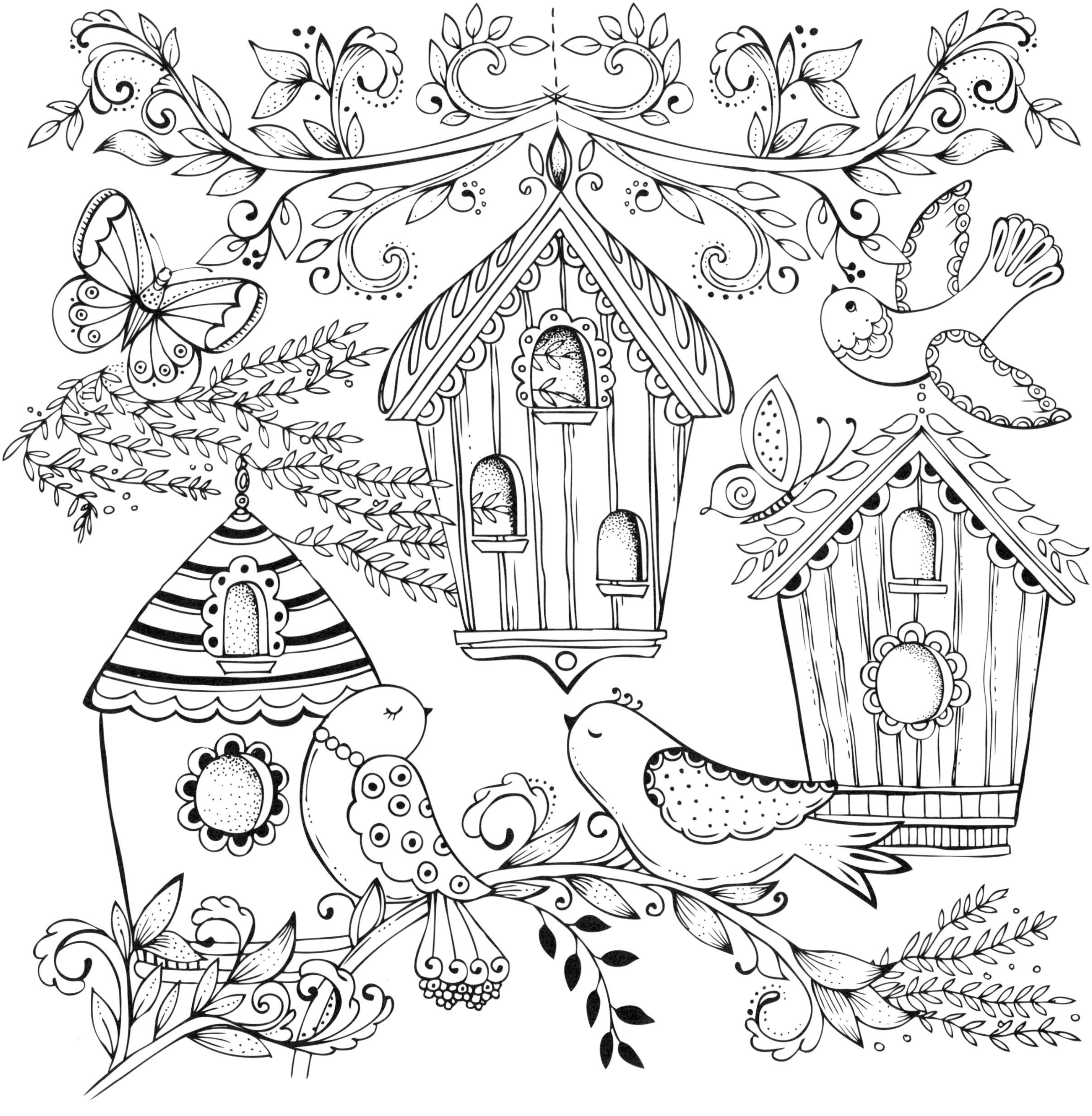

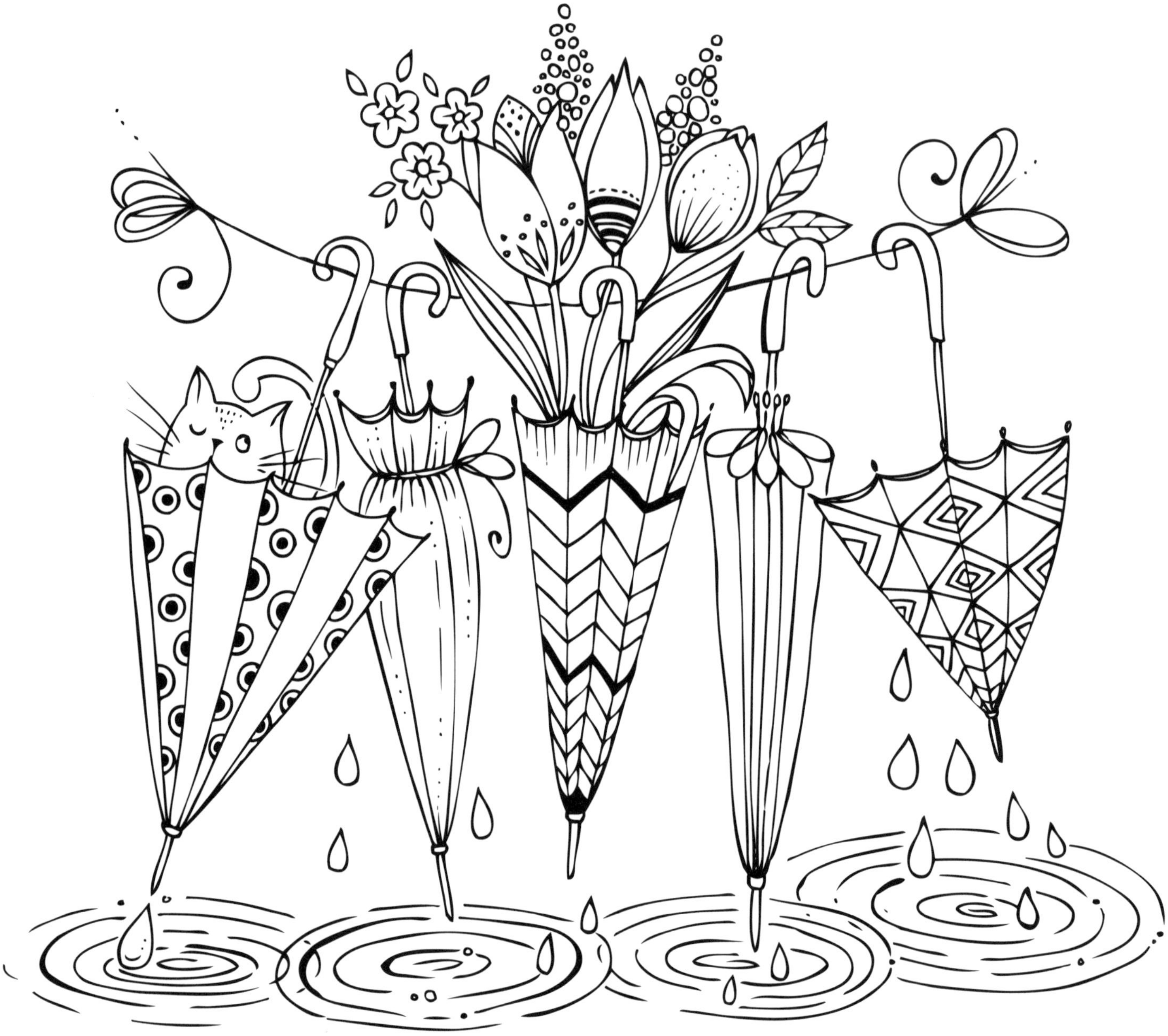

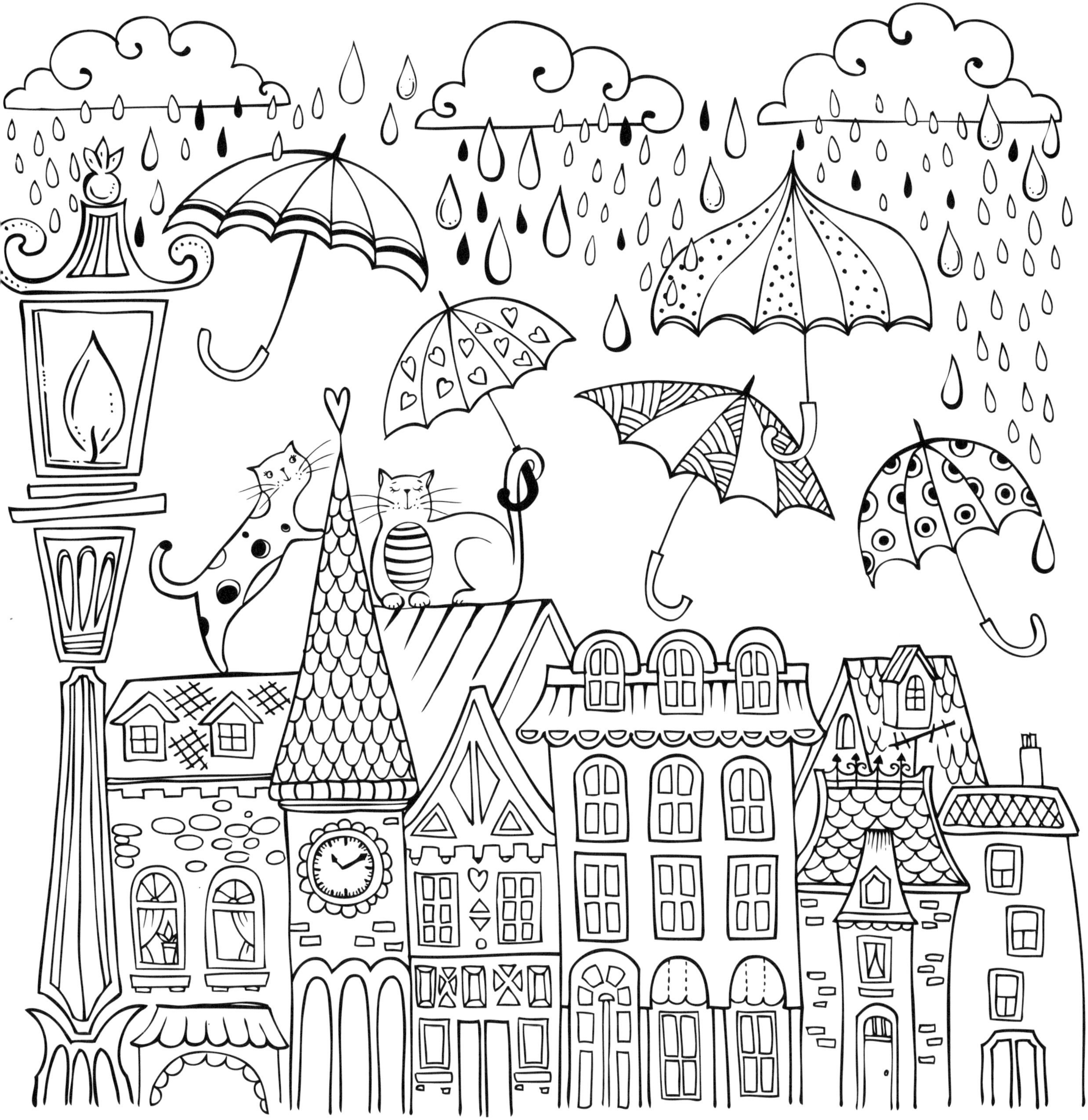

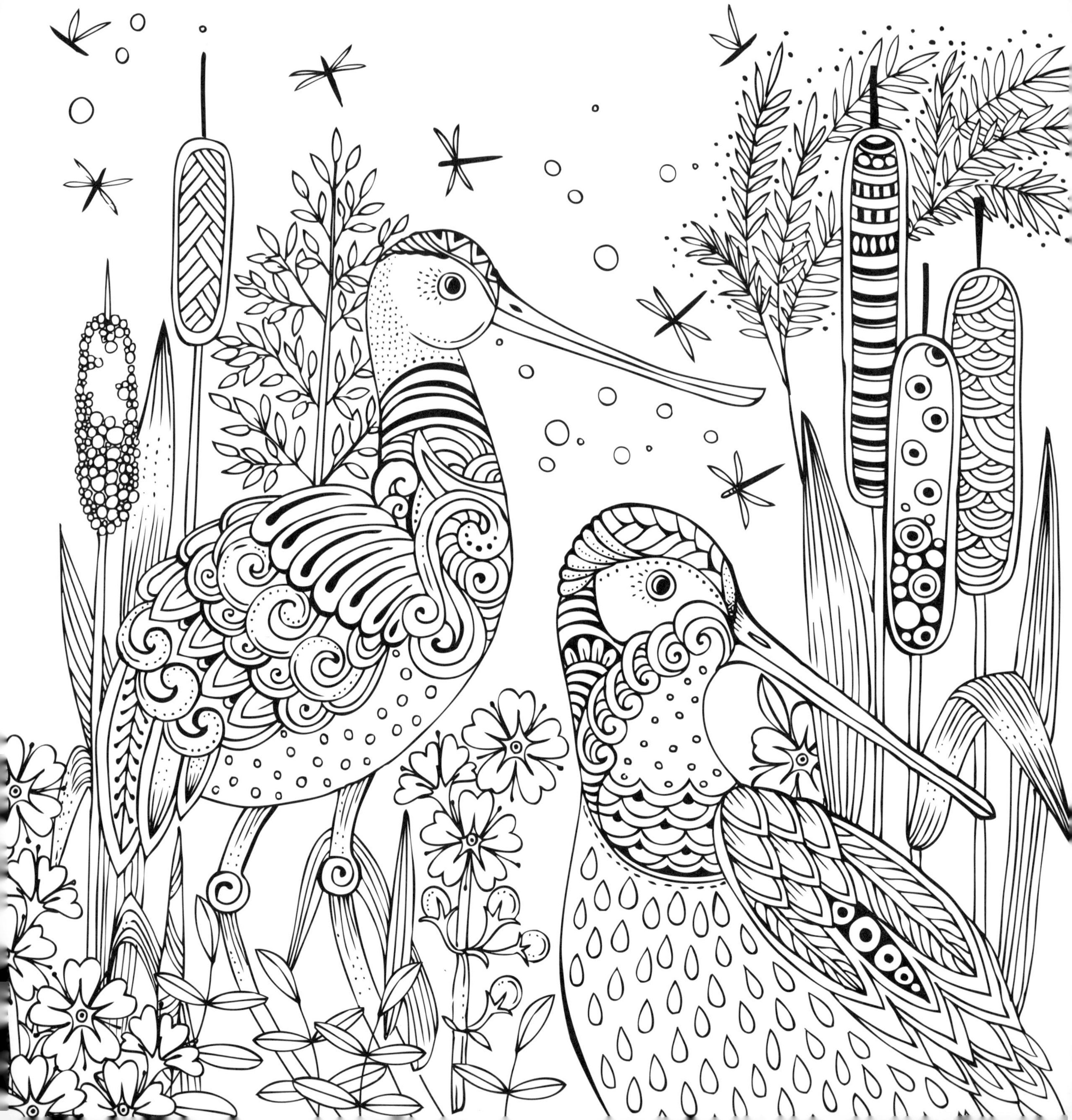

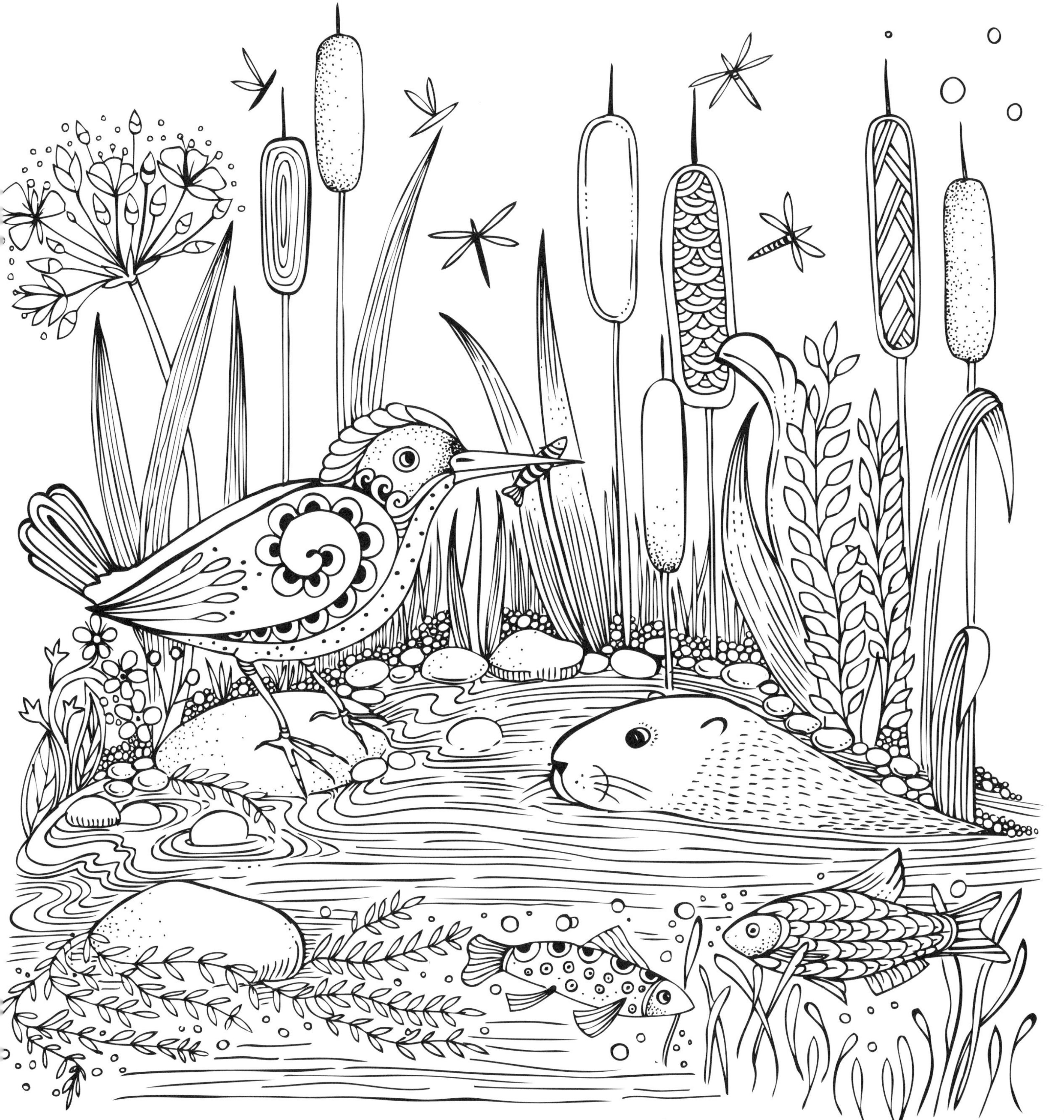

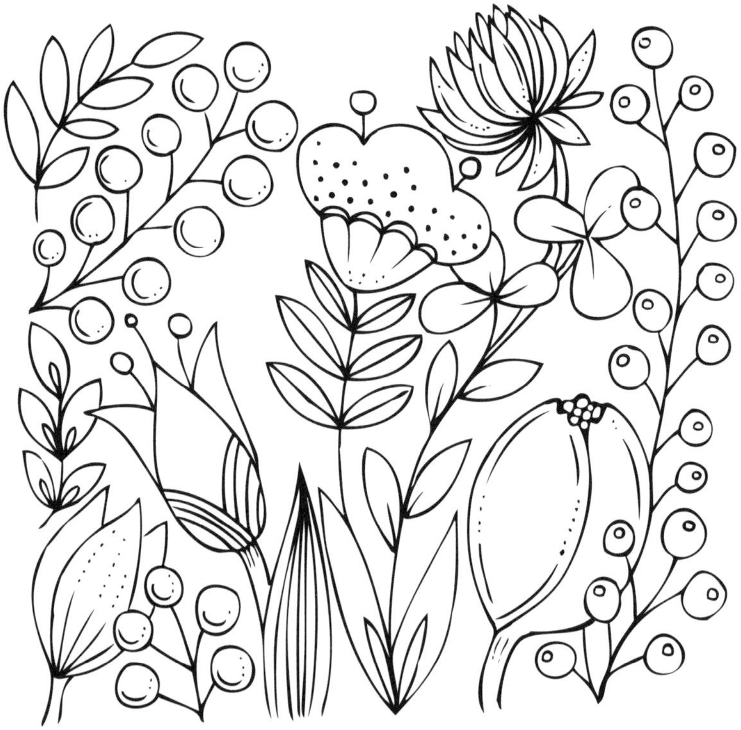
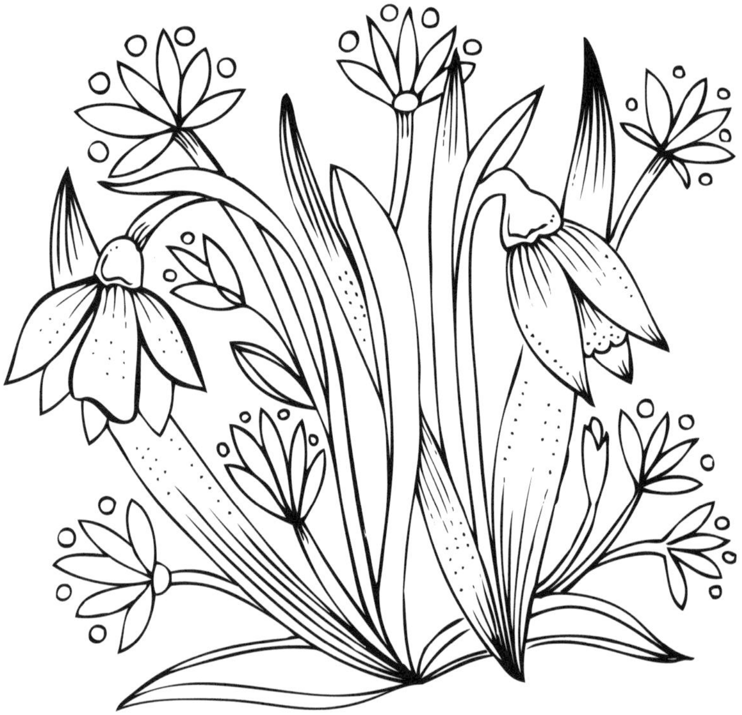
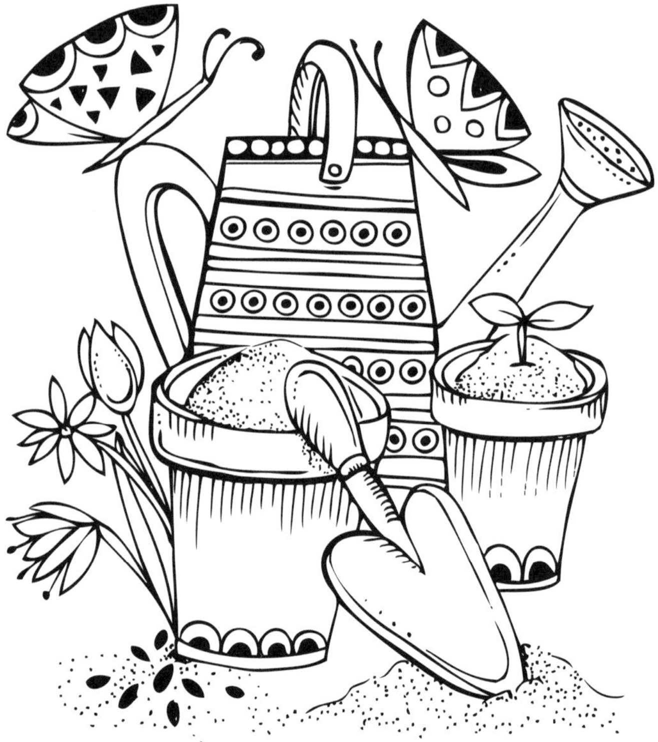
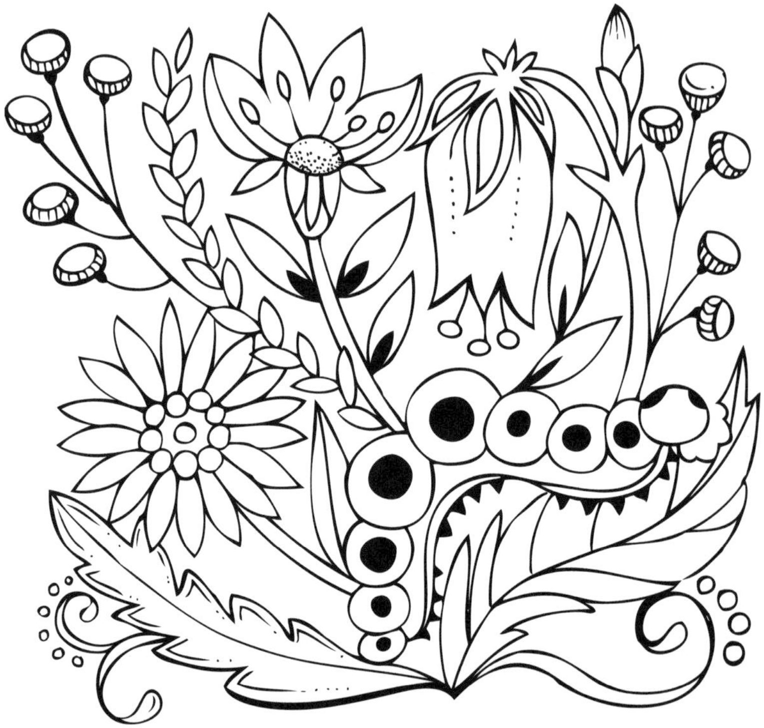

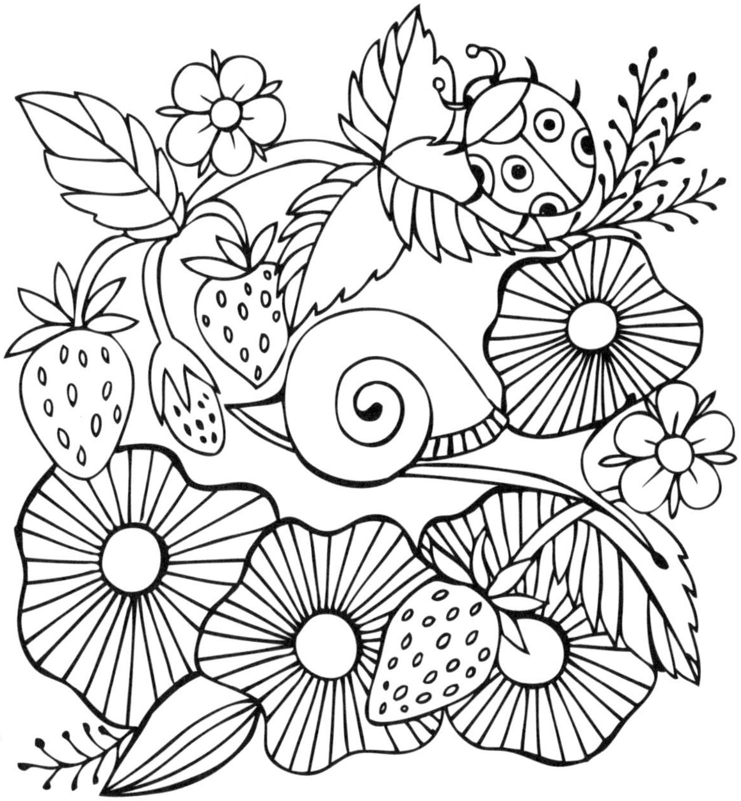

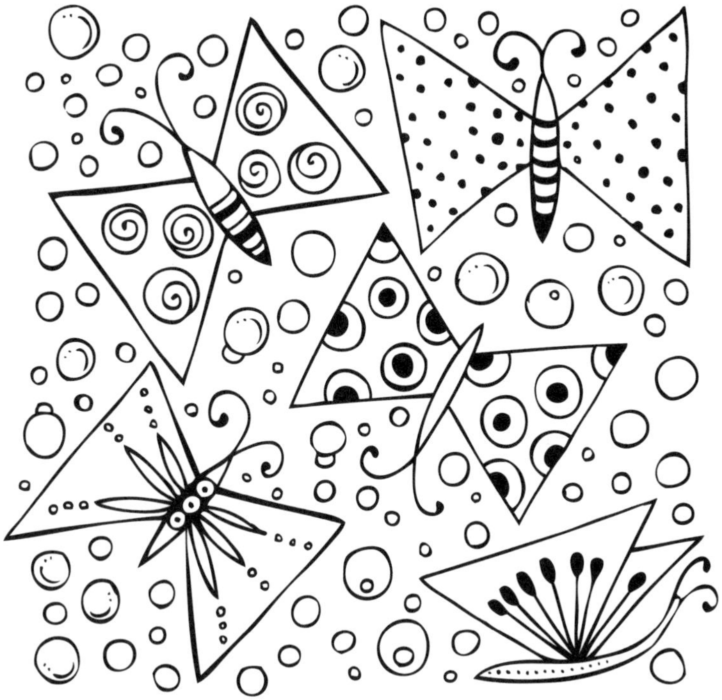

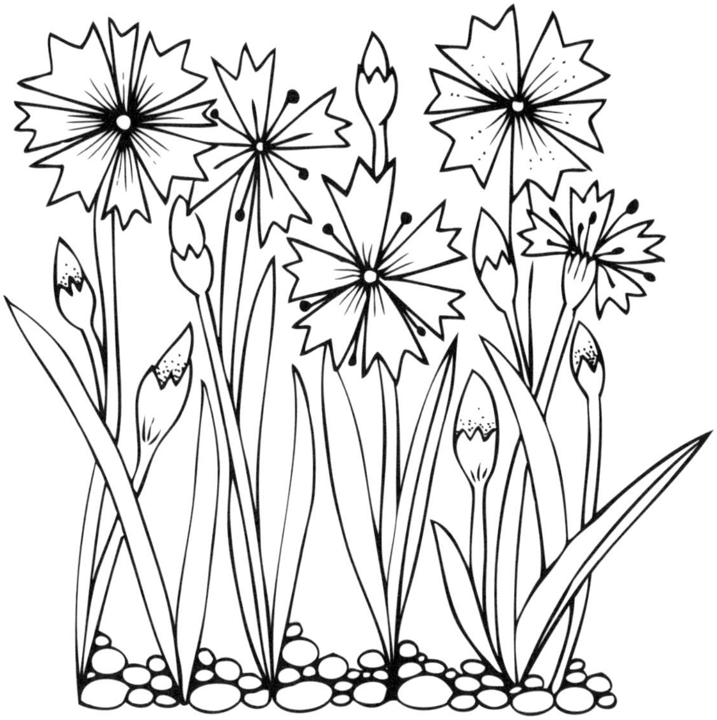

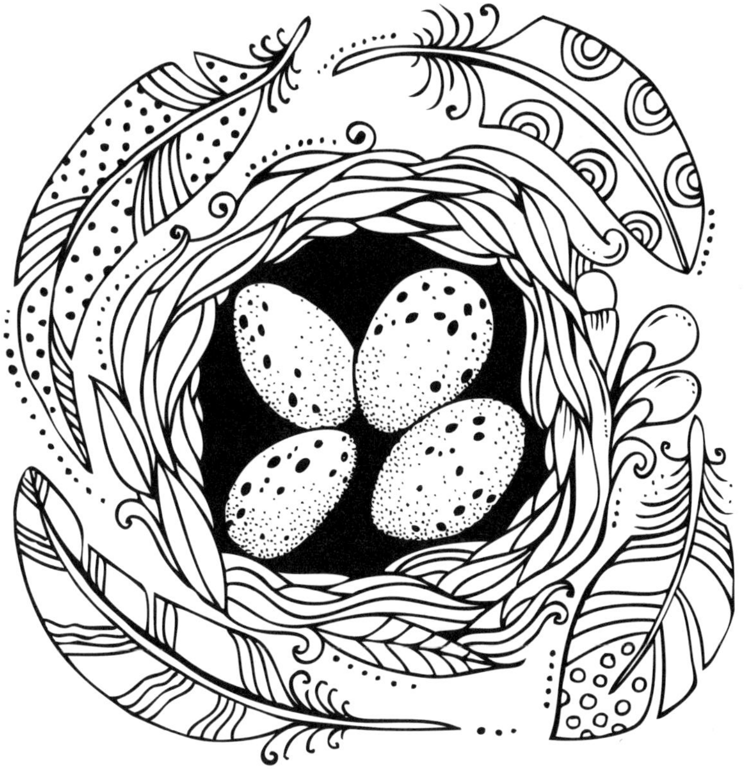

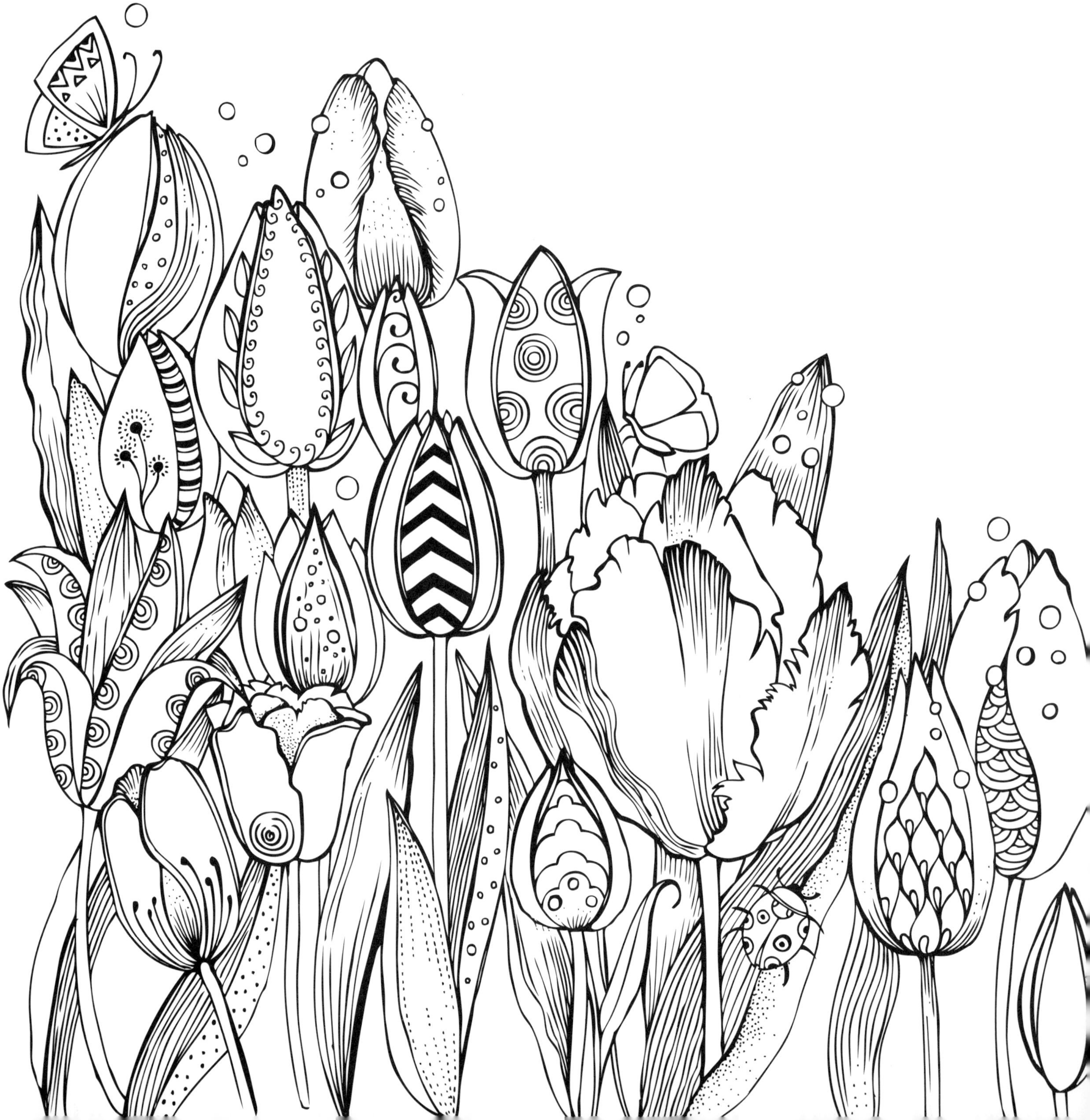

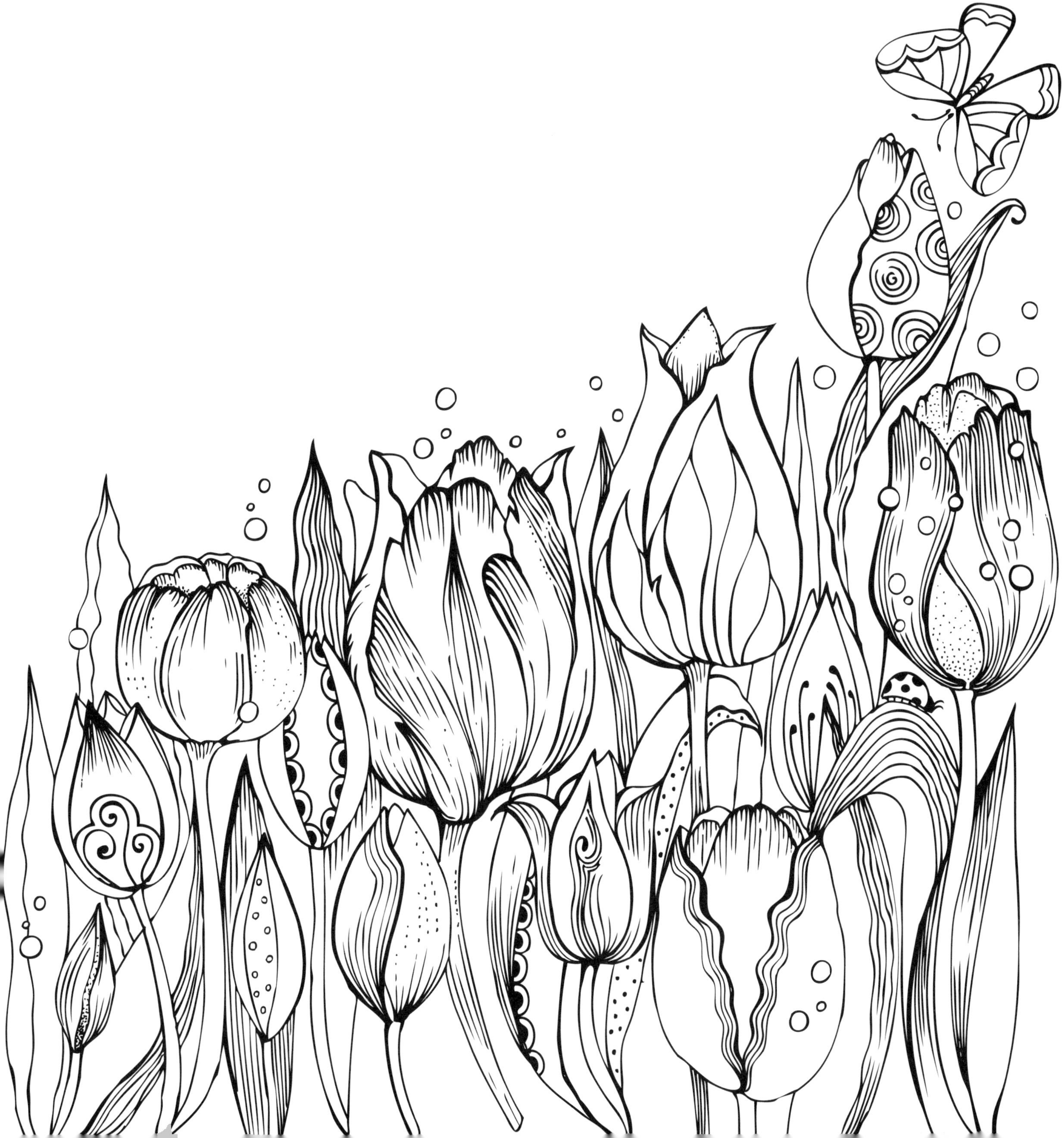

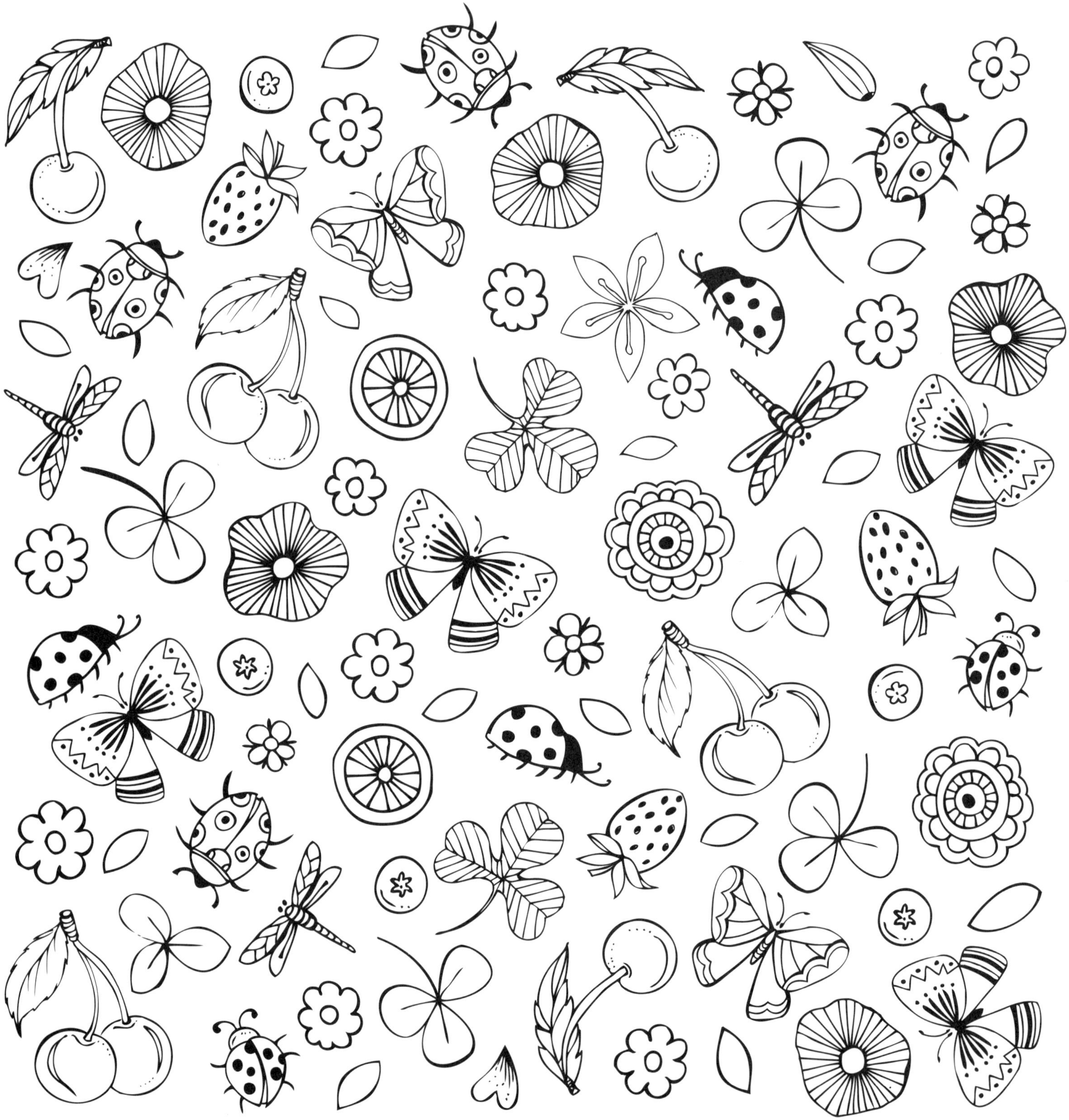

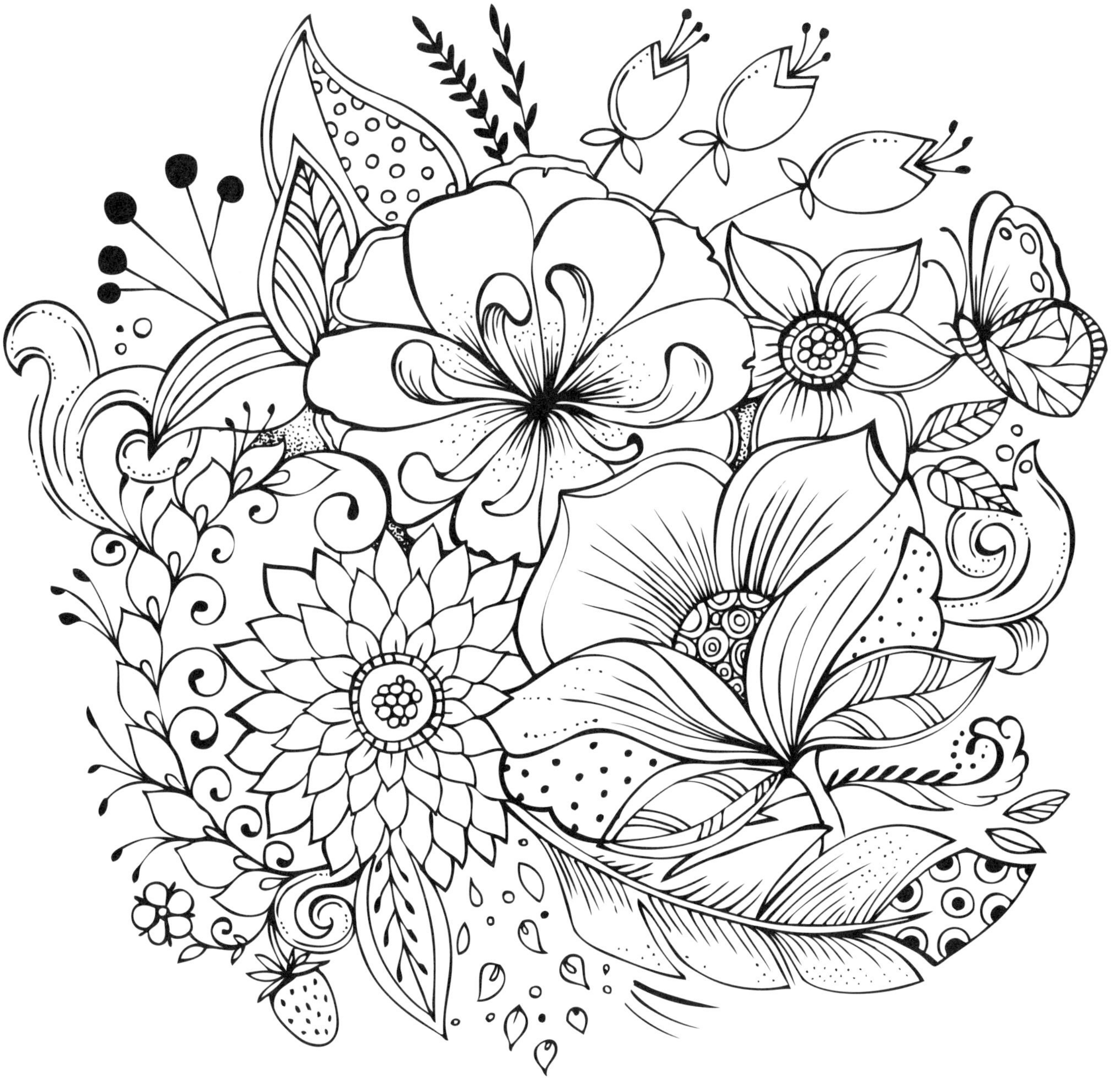

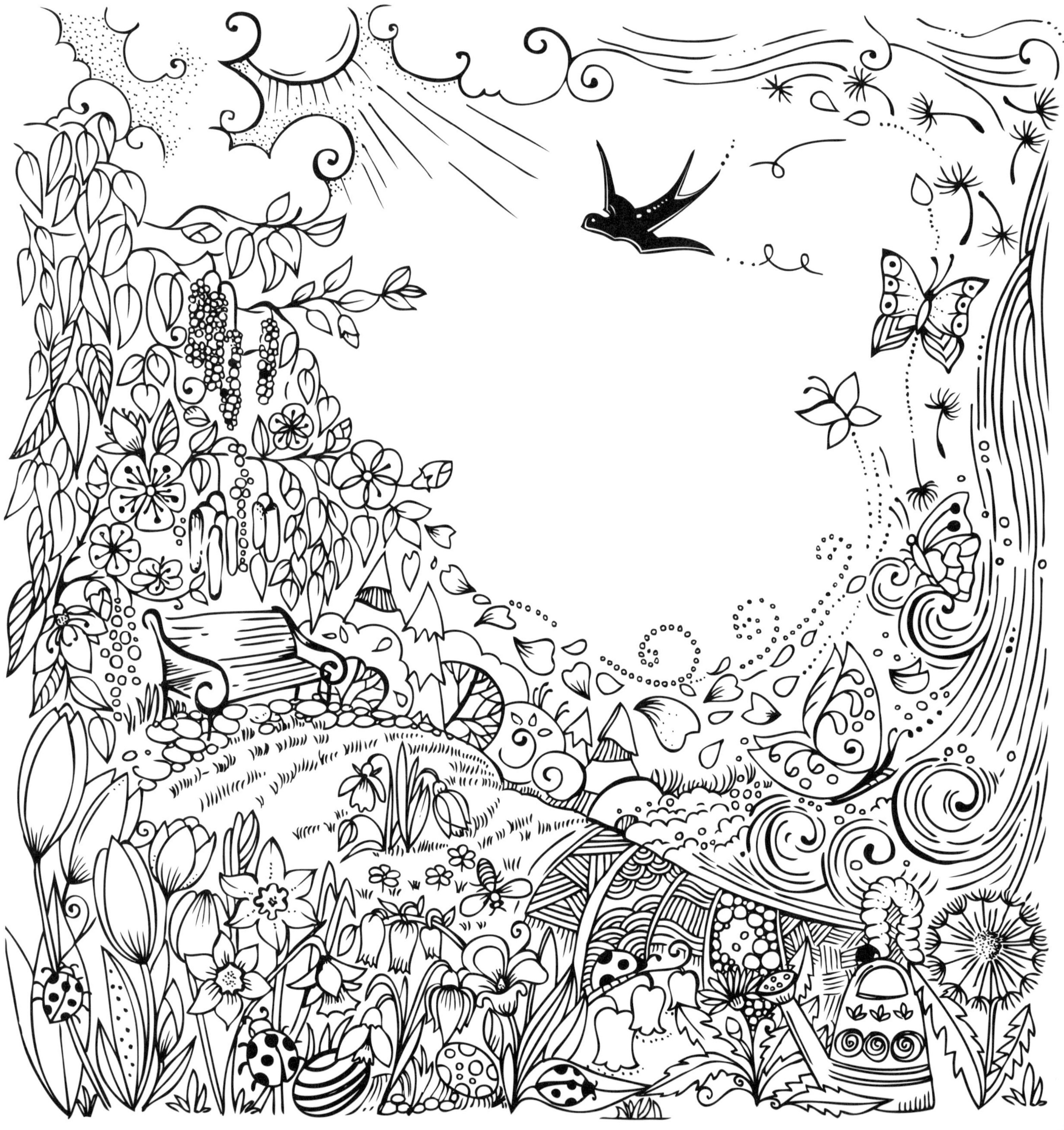

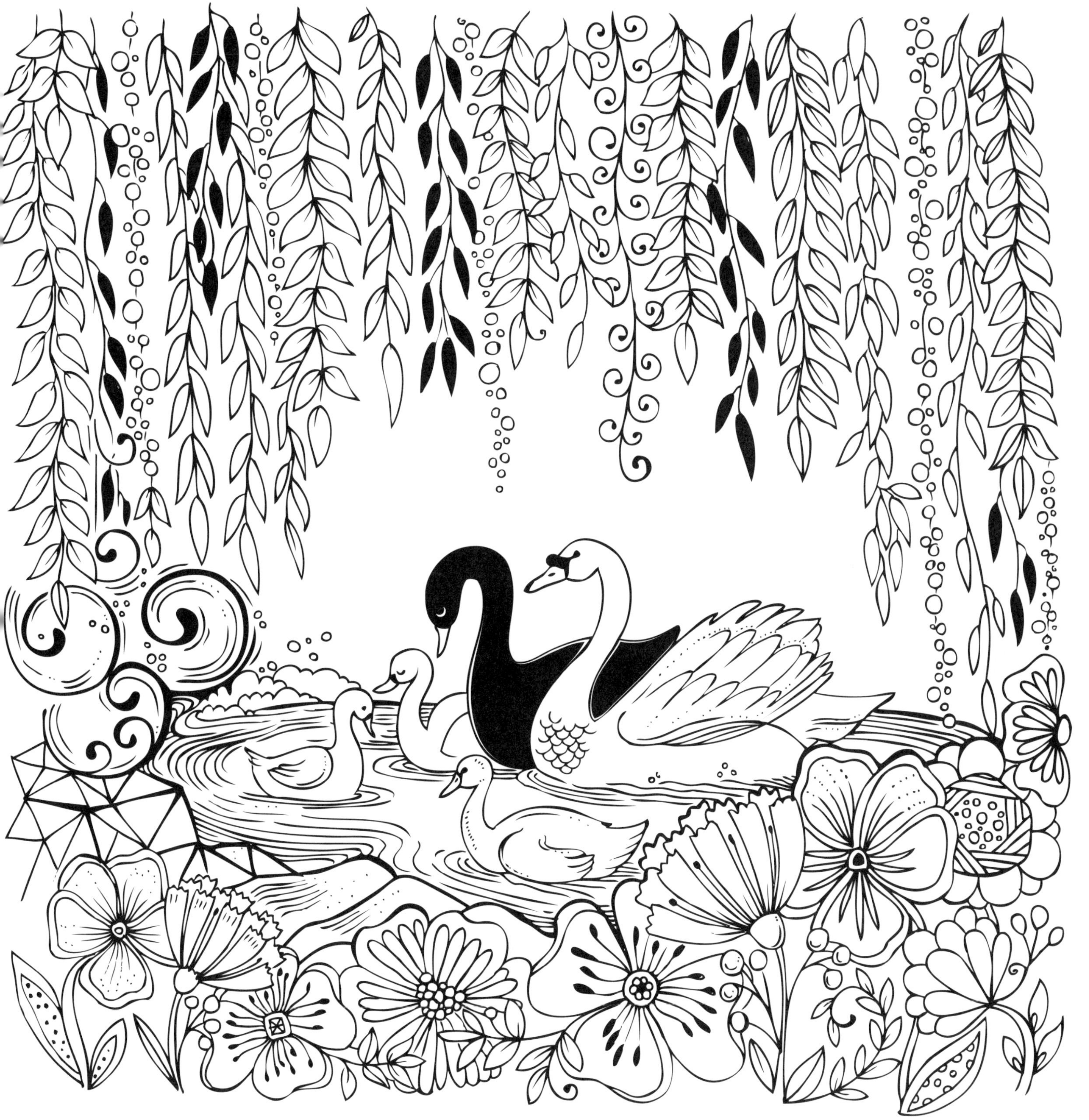

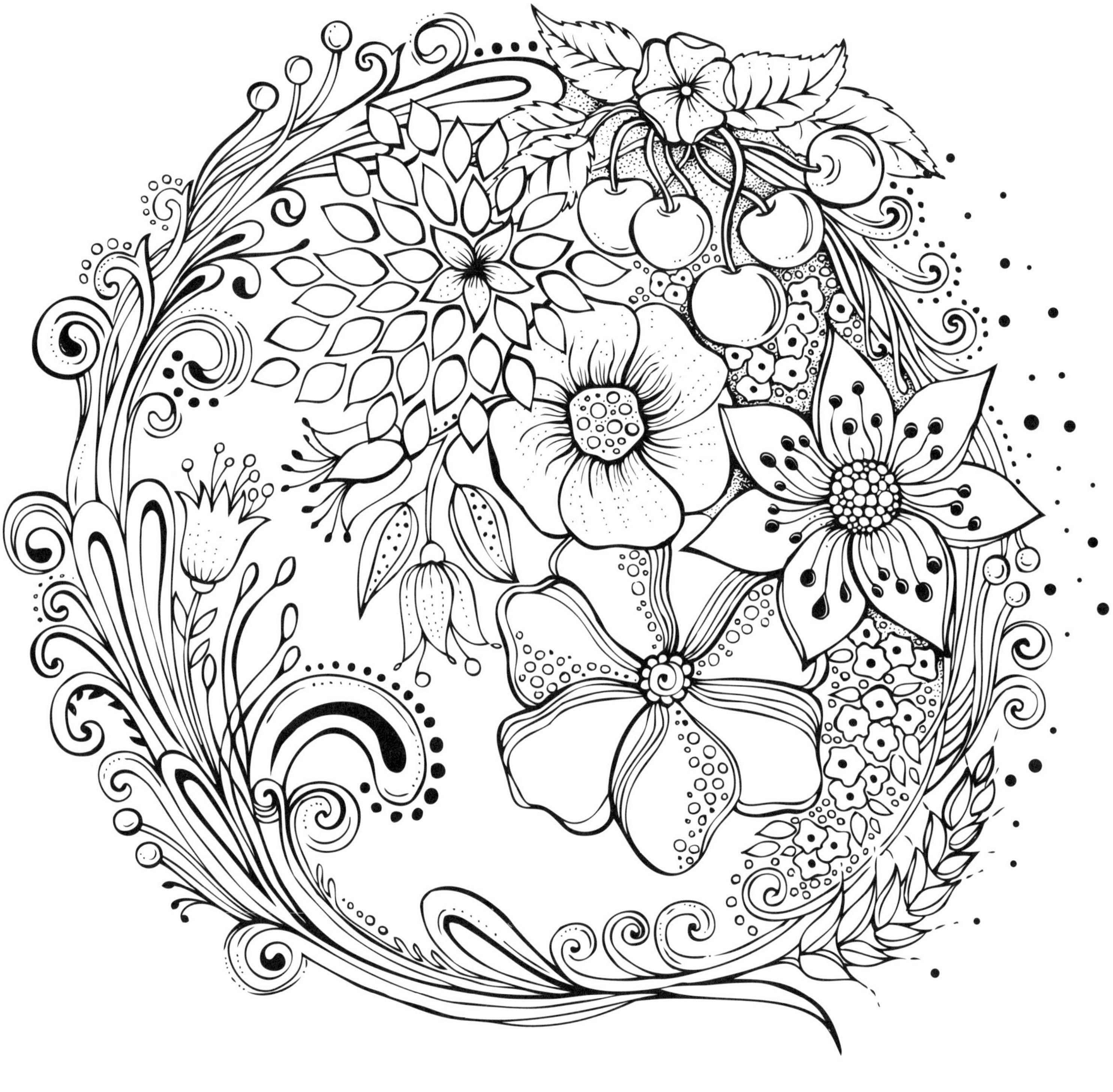

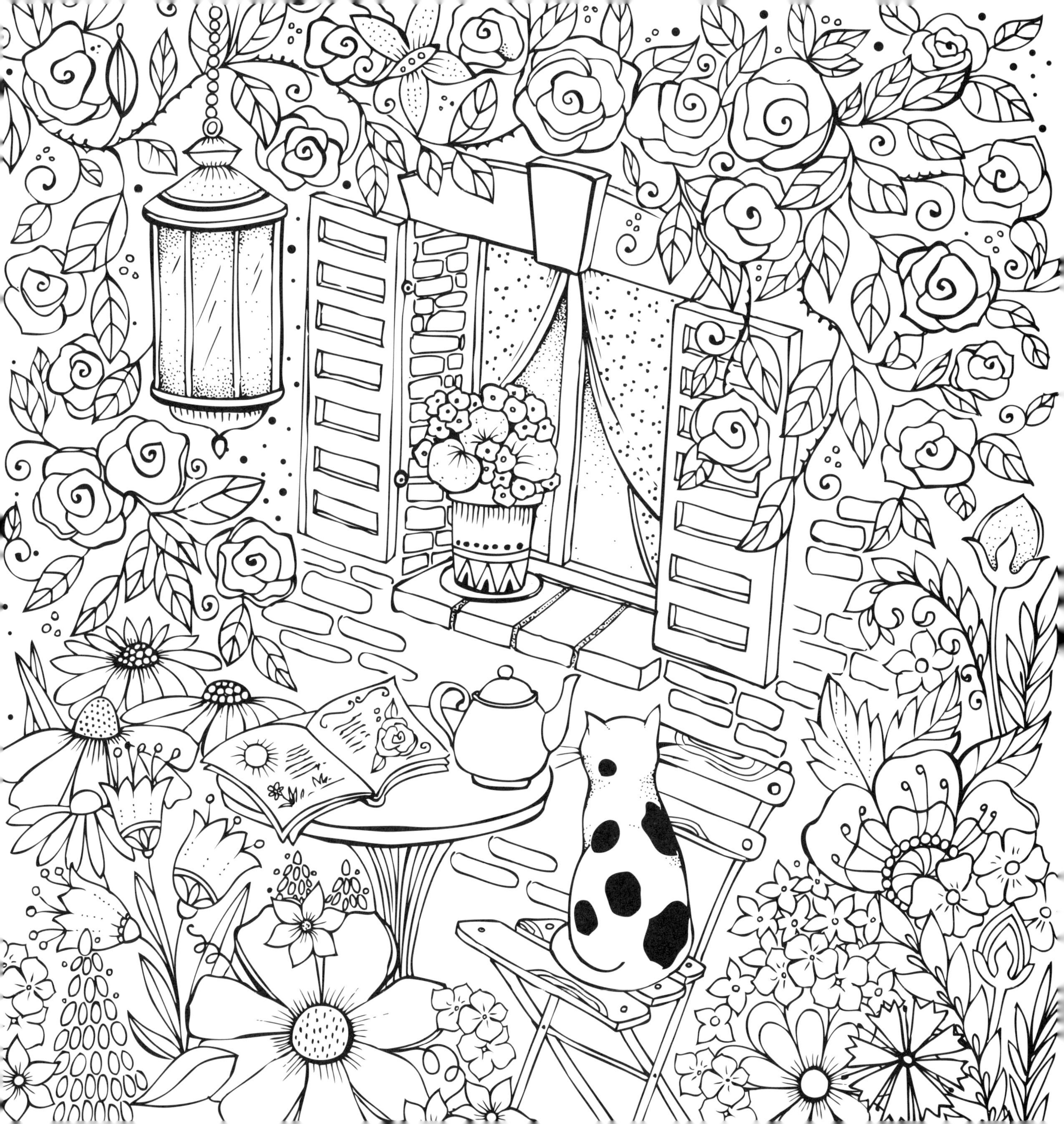

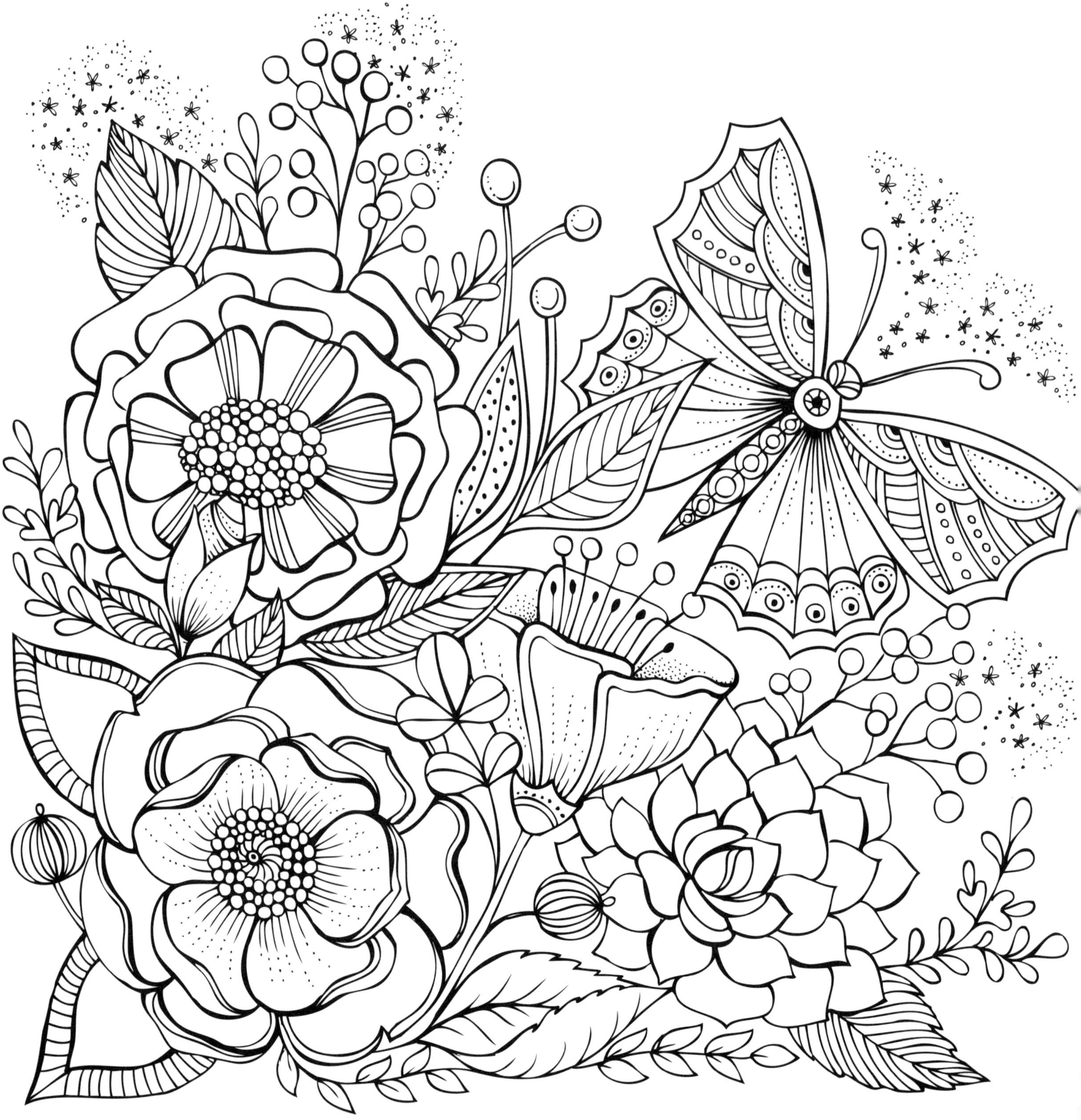

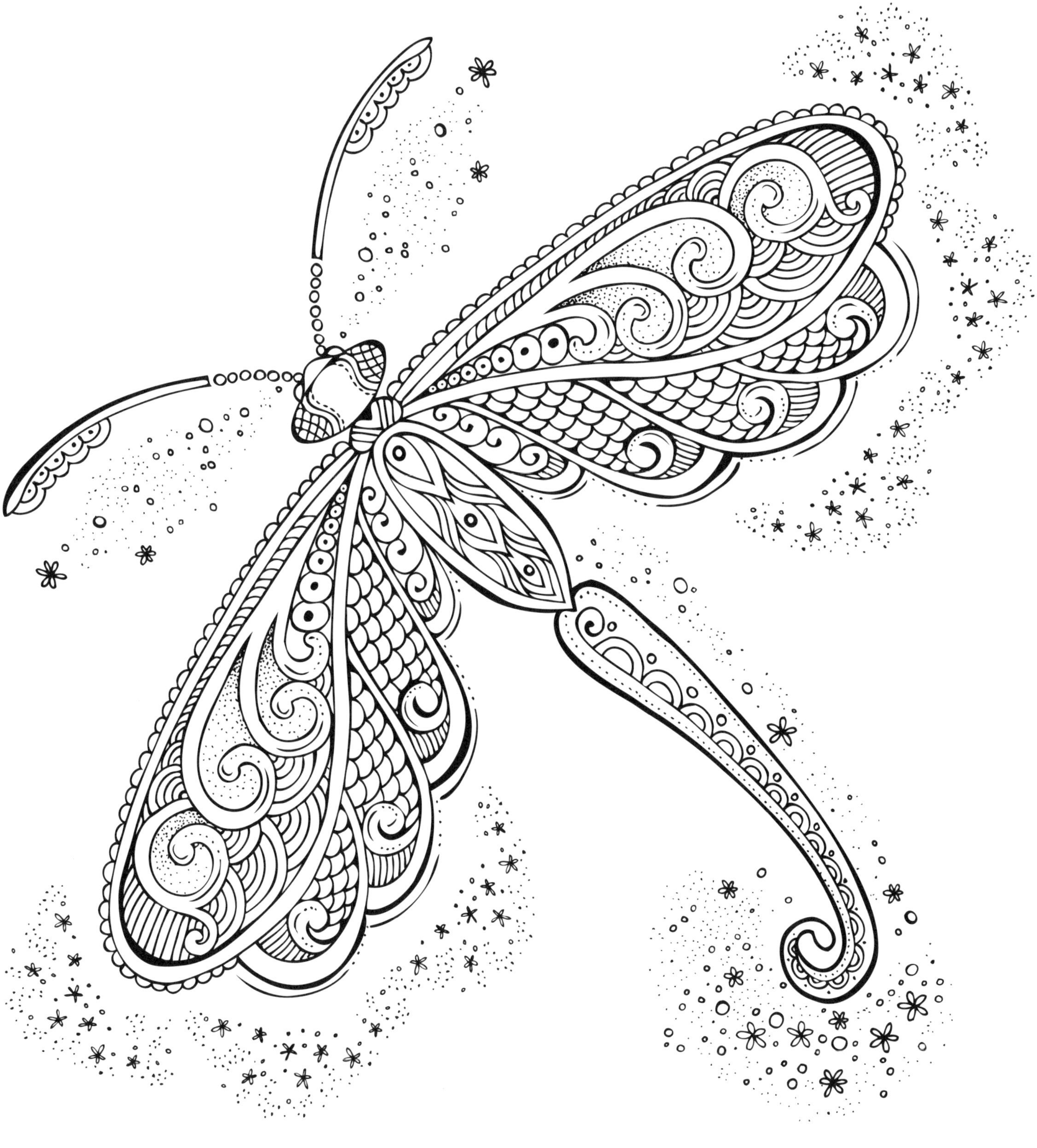

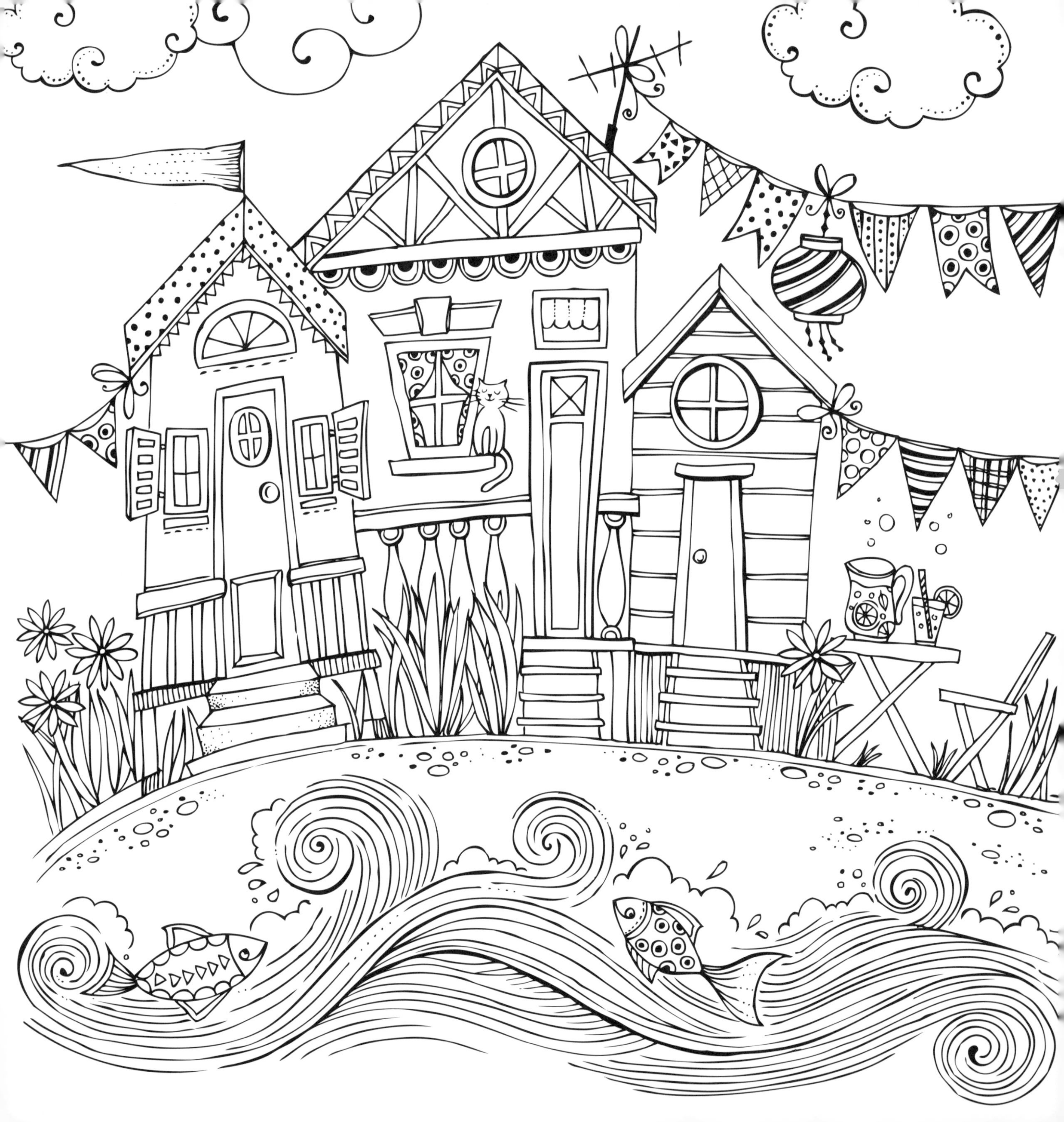

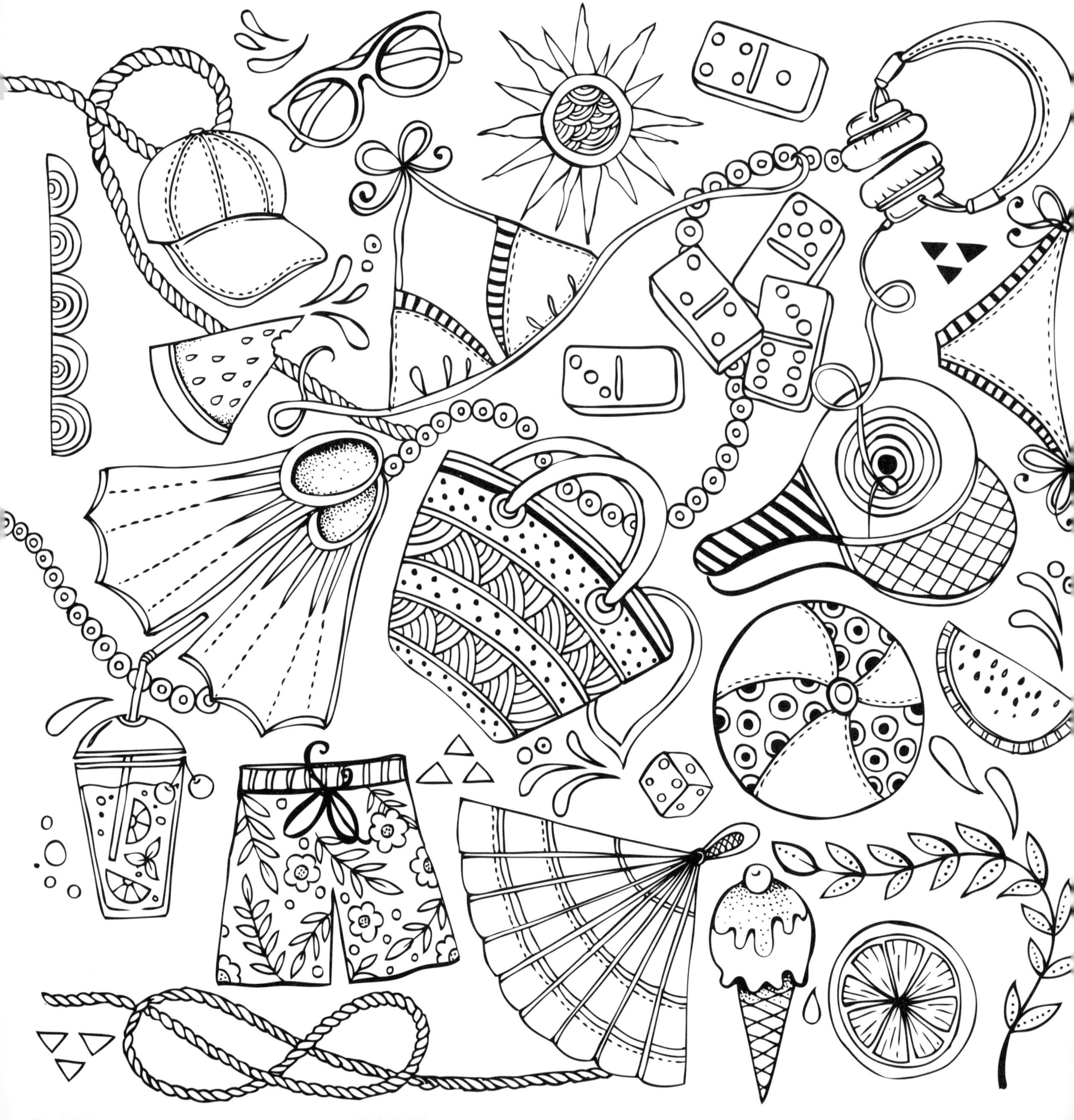

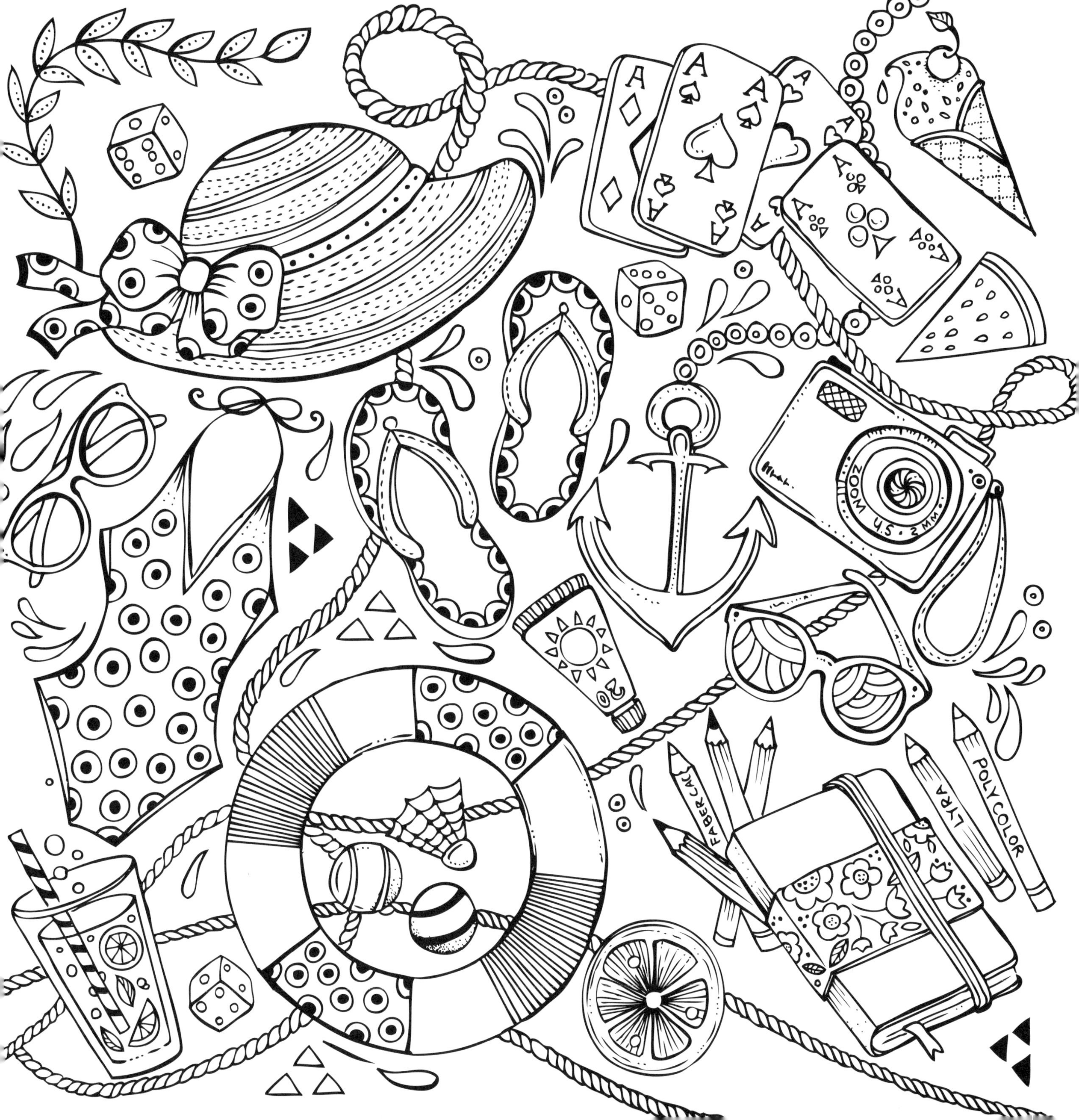
LYRA
POLYCOLOR

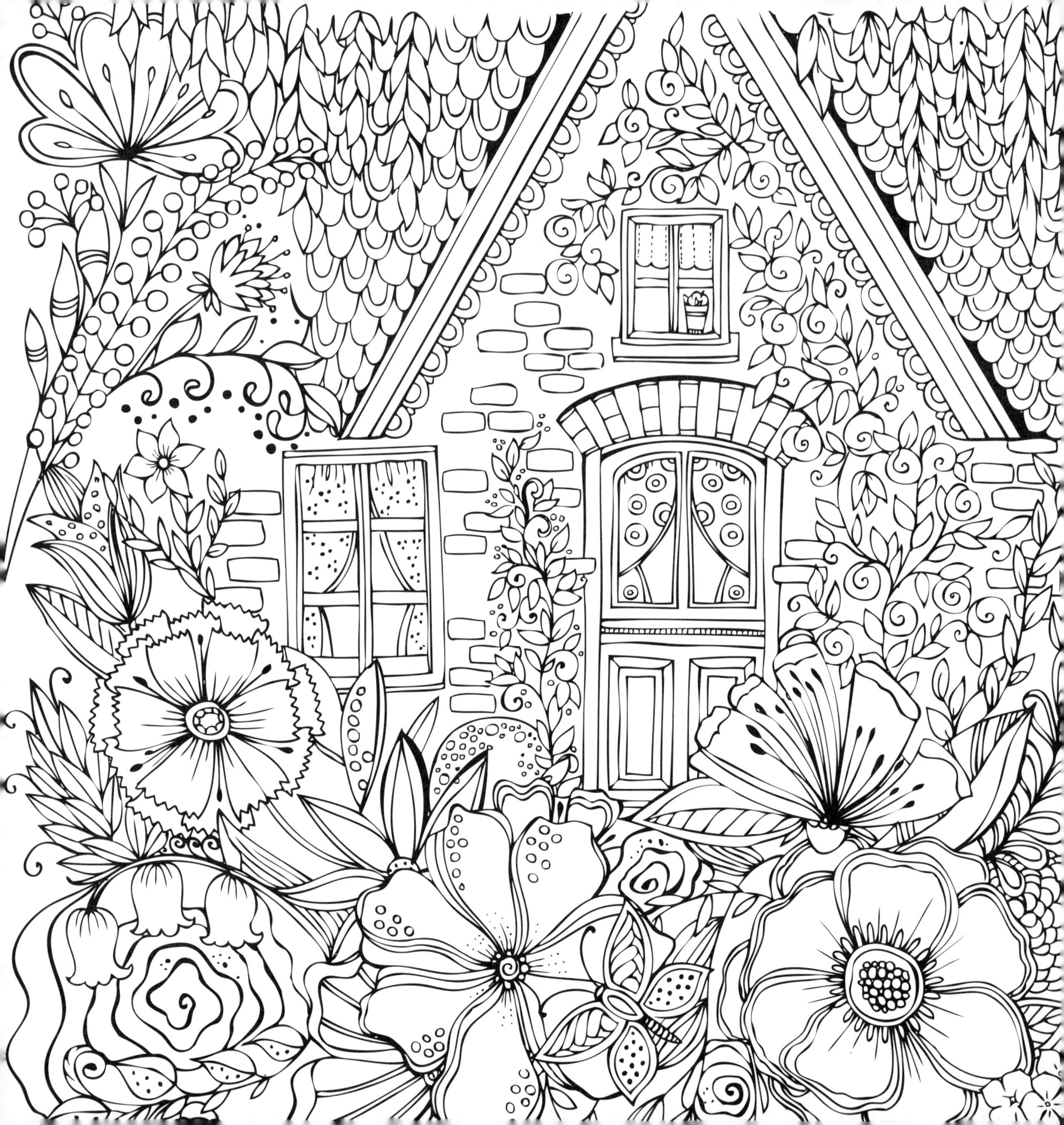

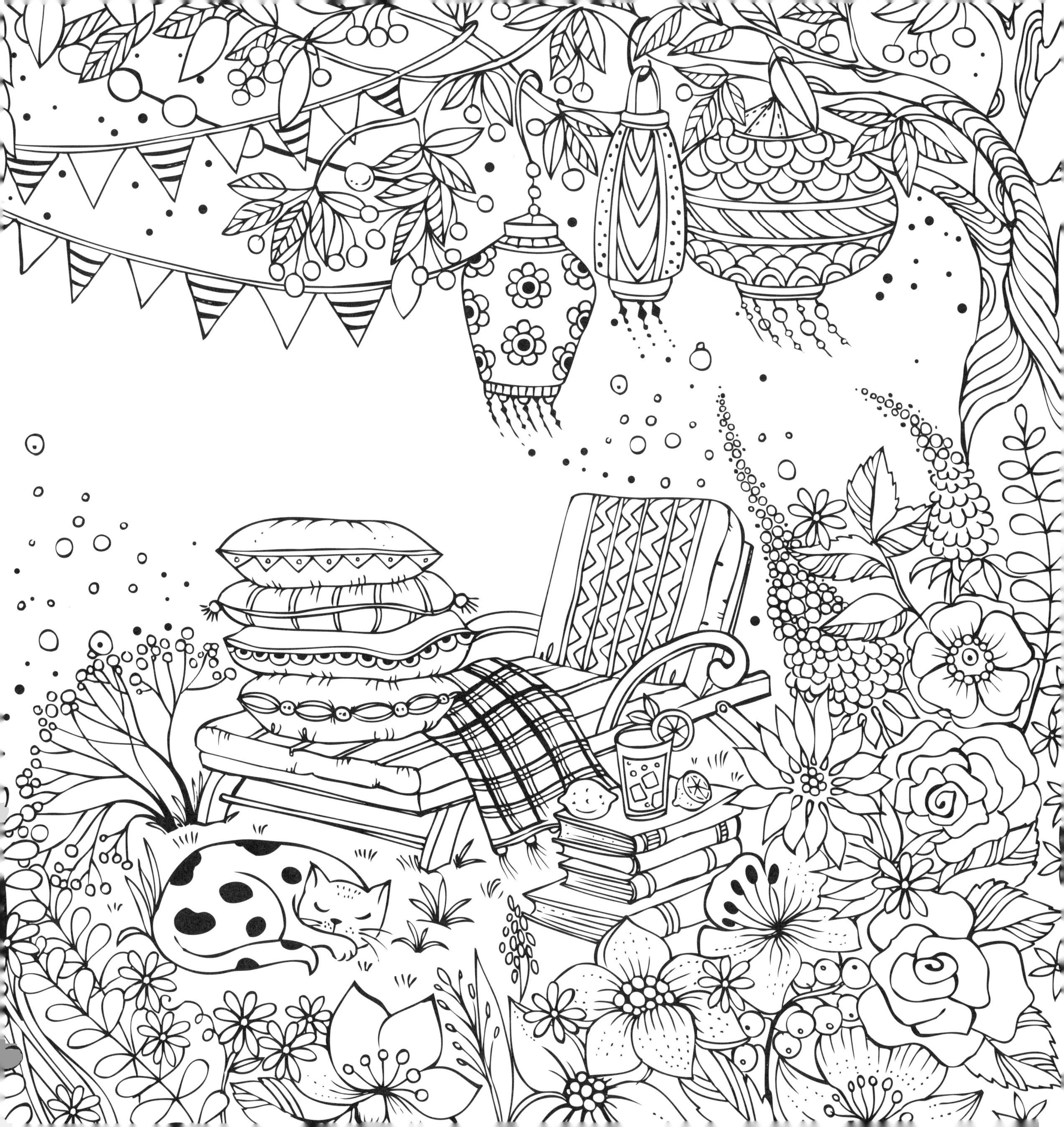

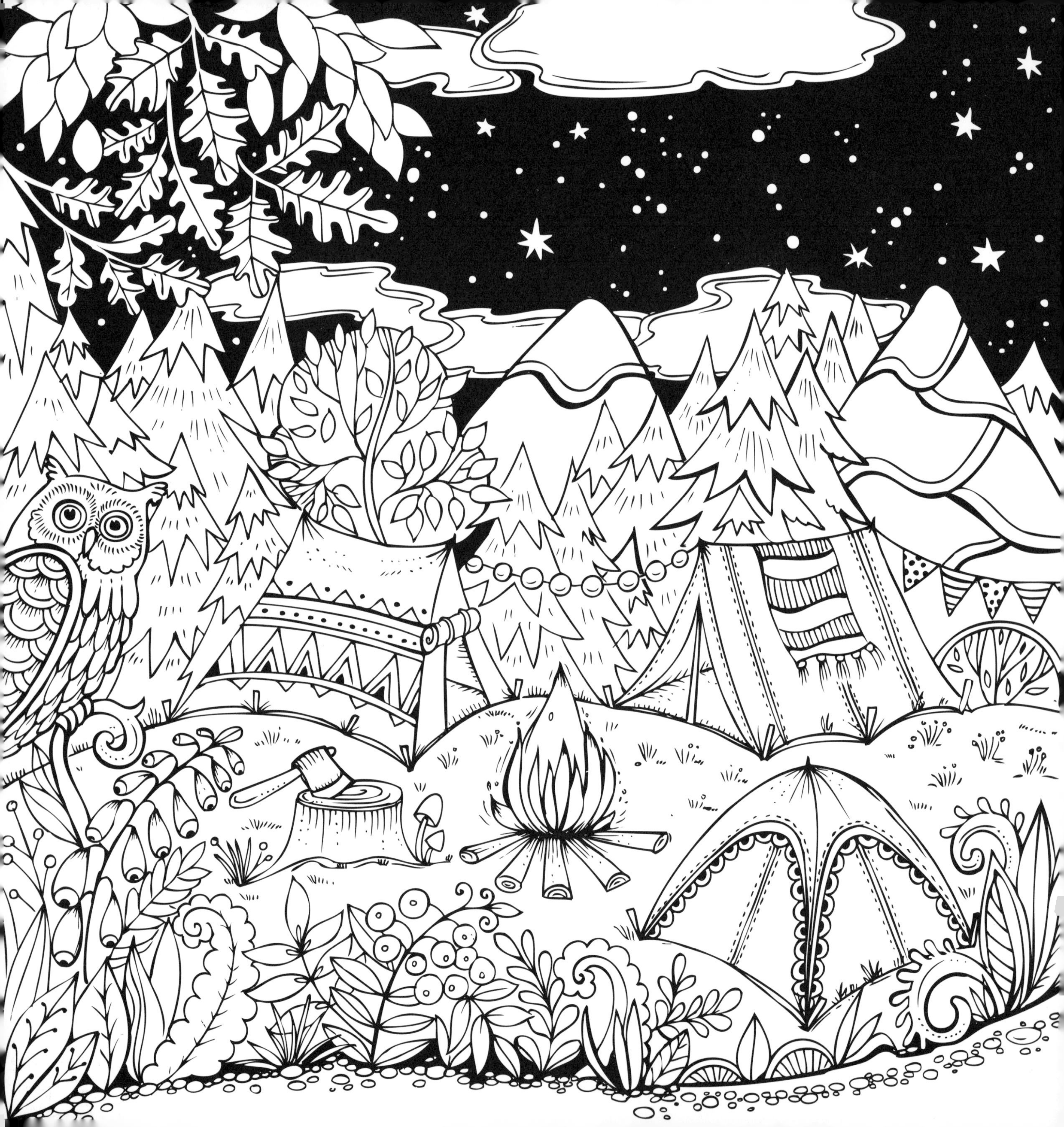

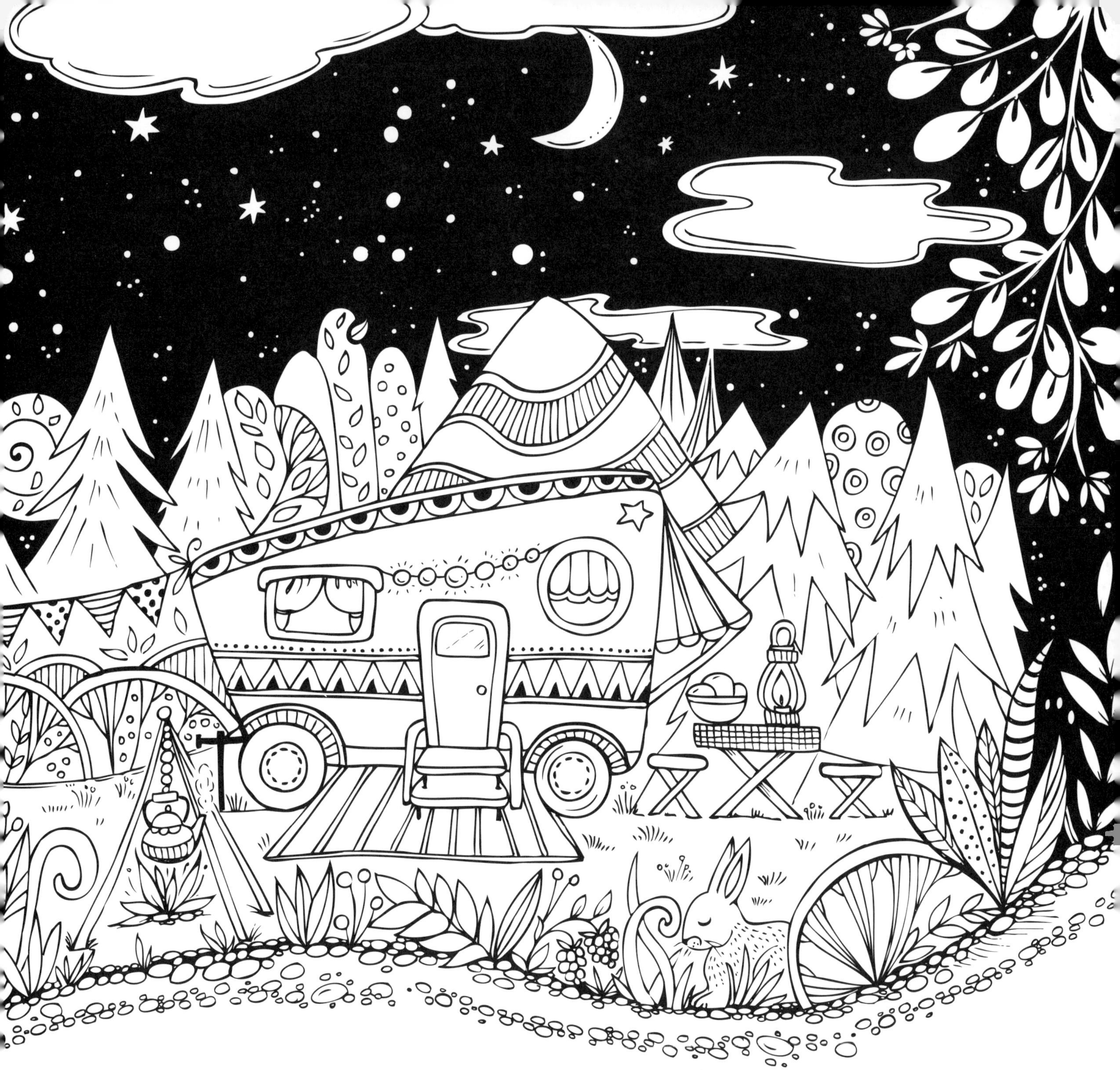

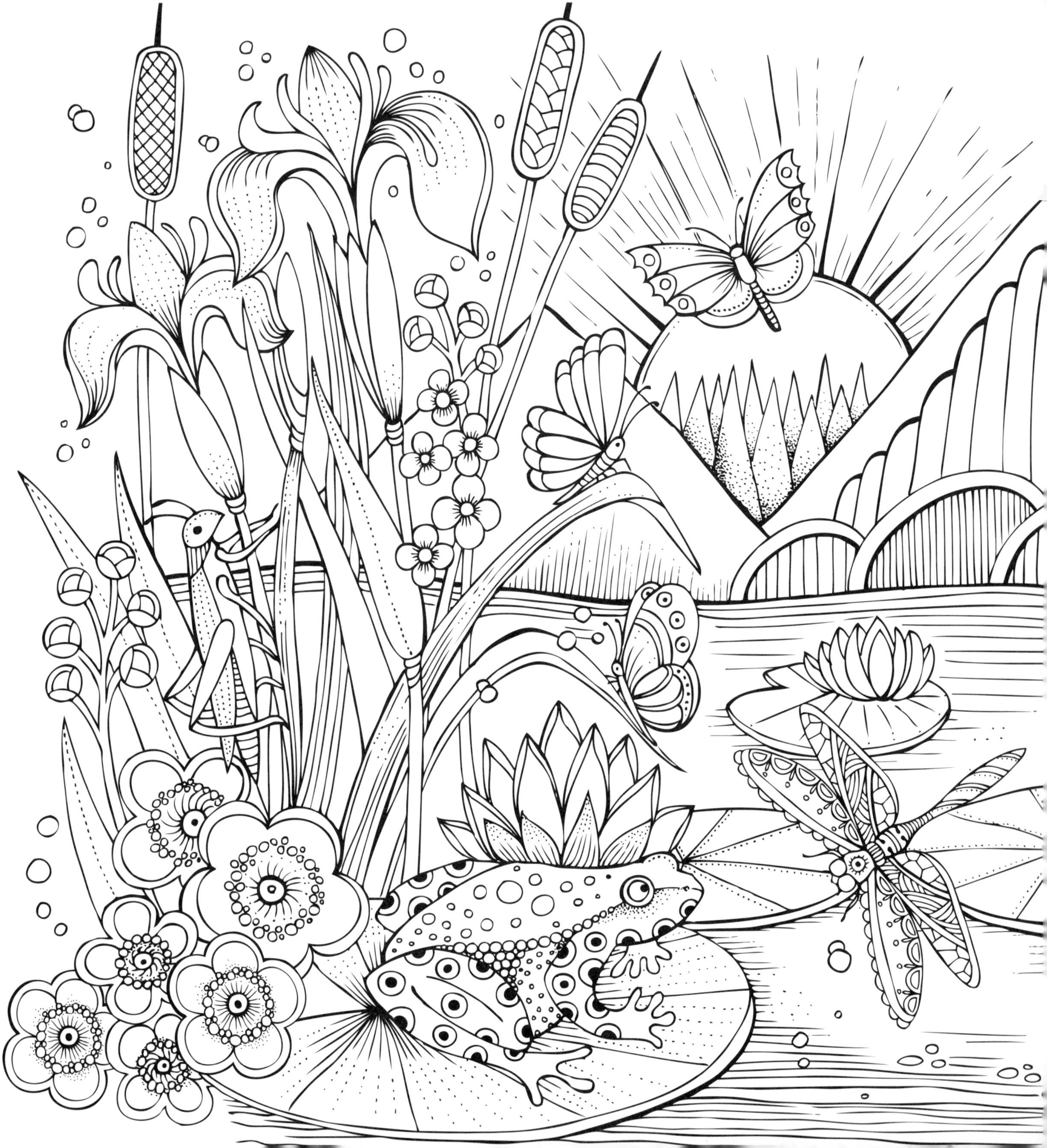

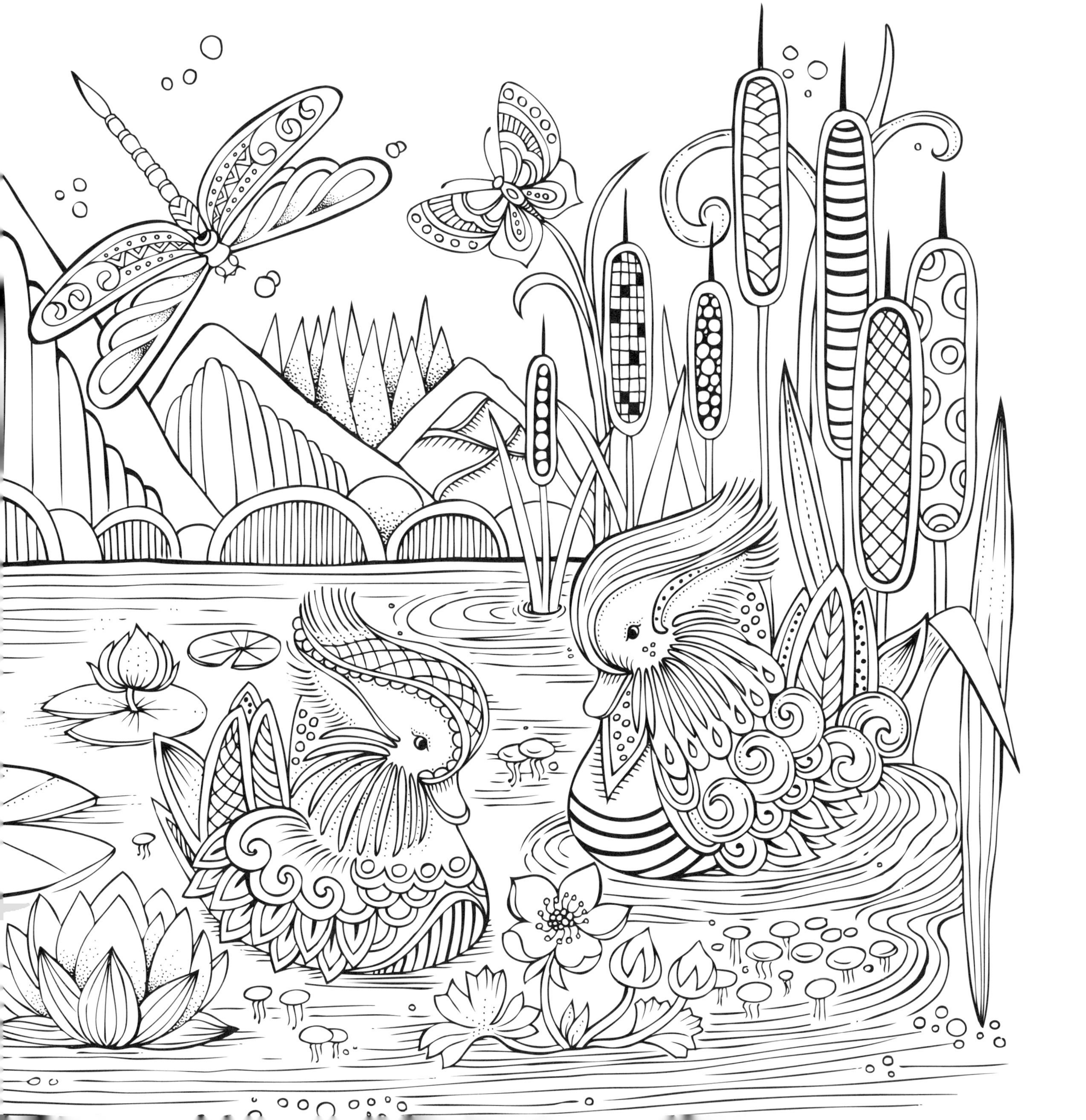

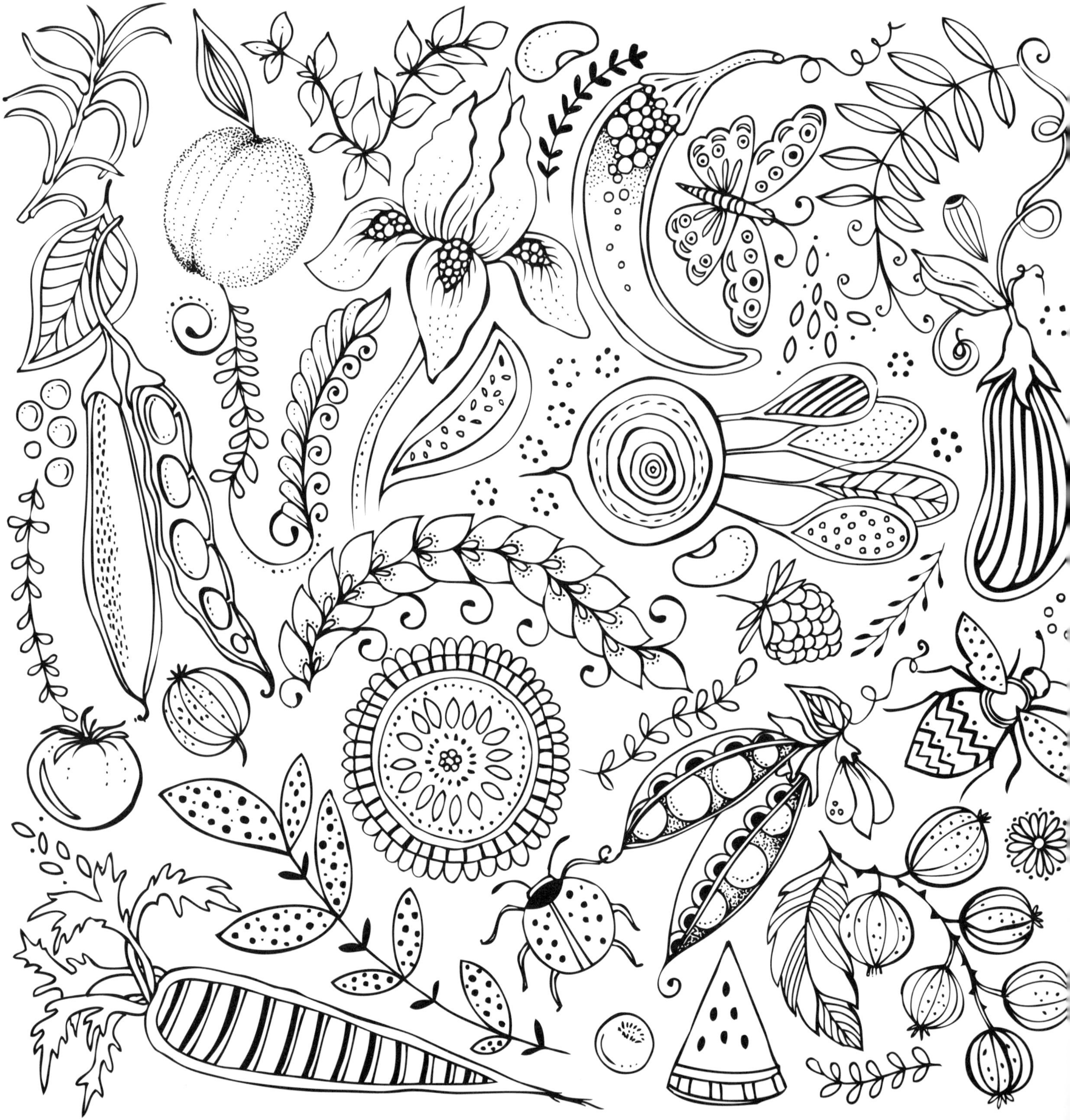

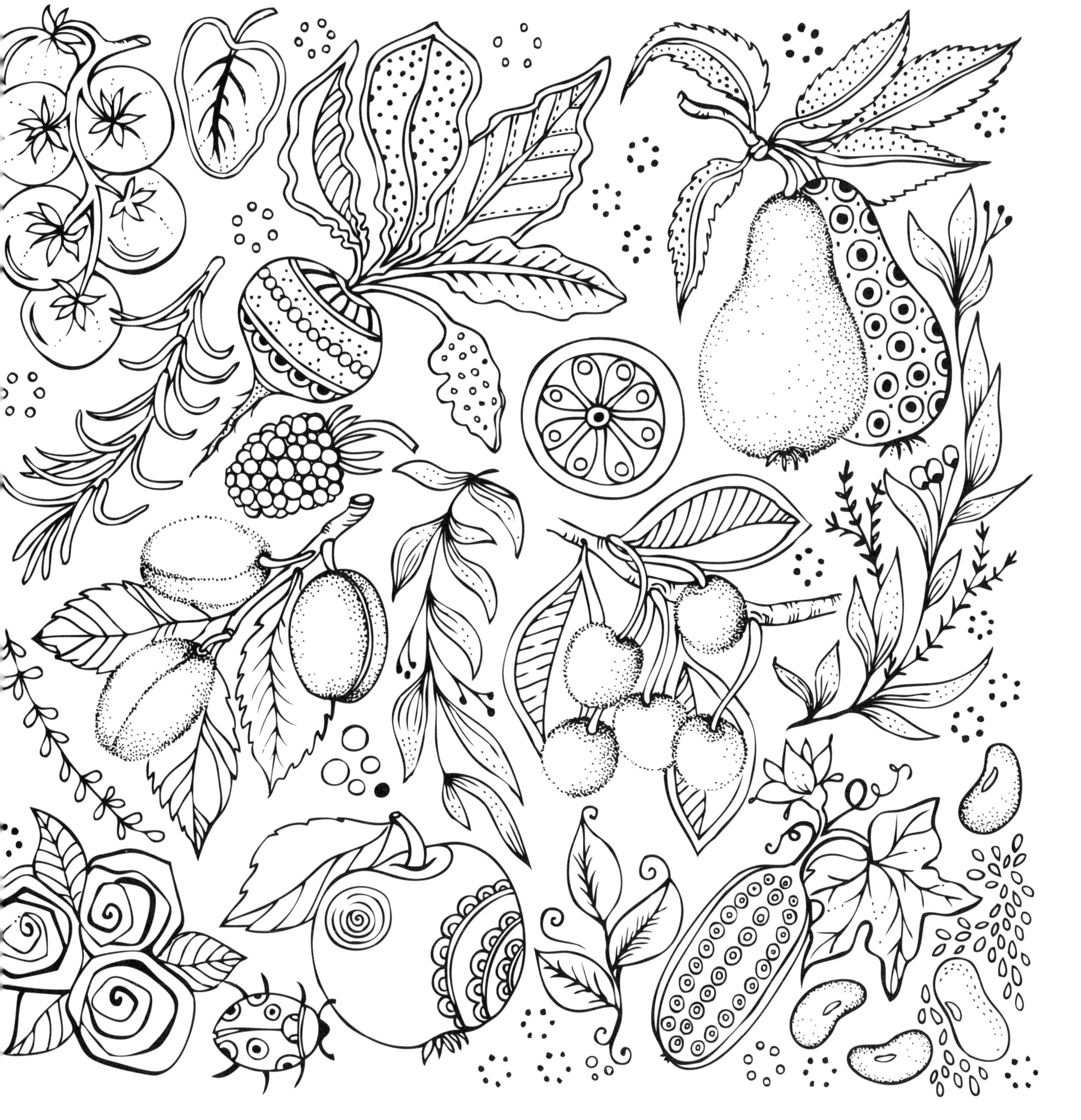

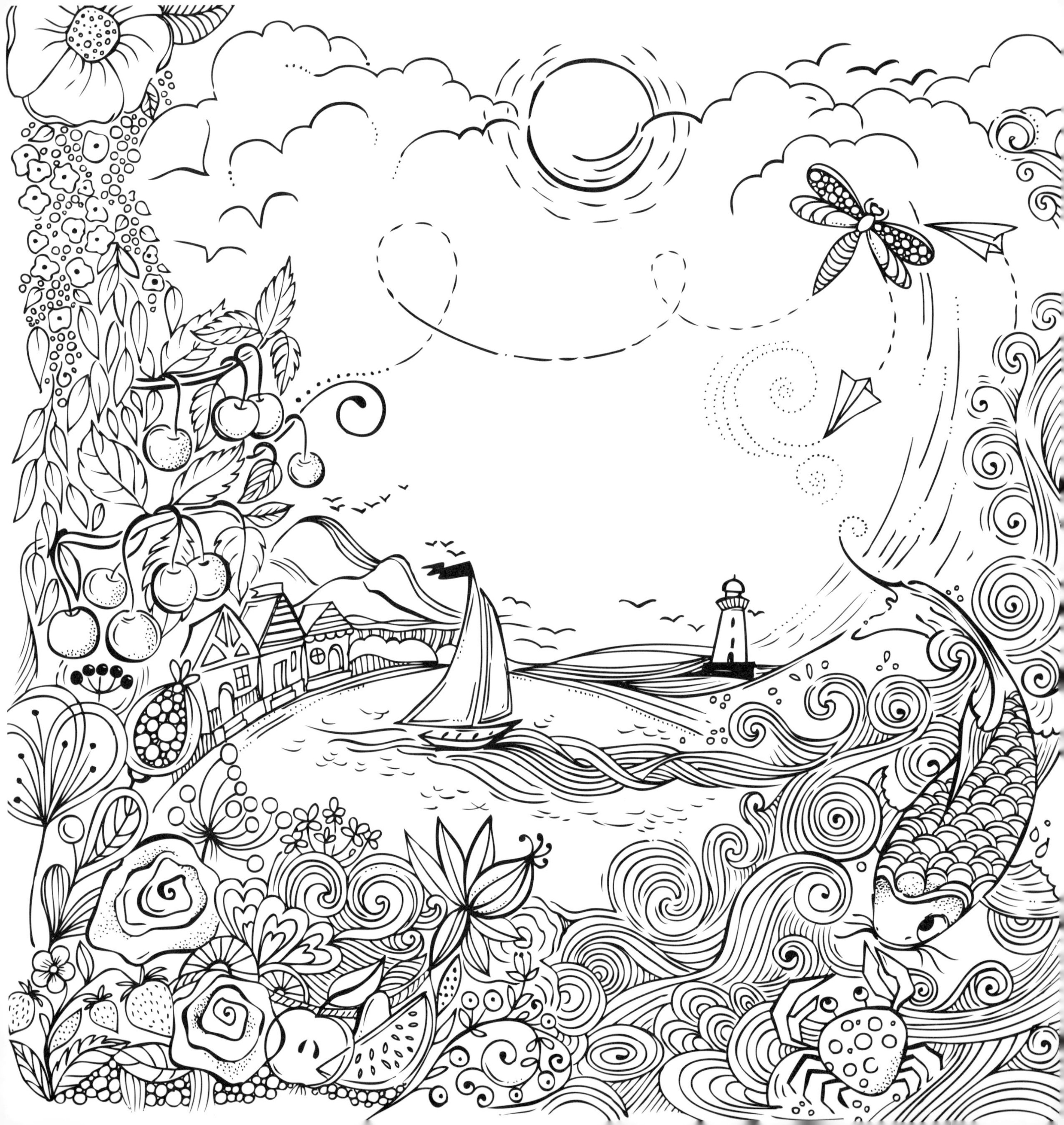

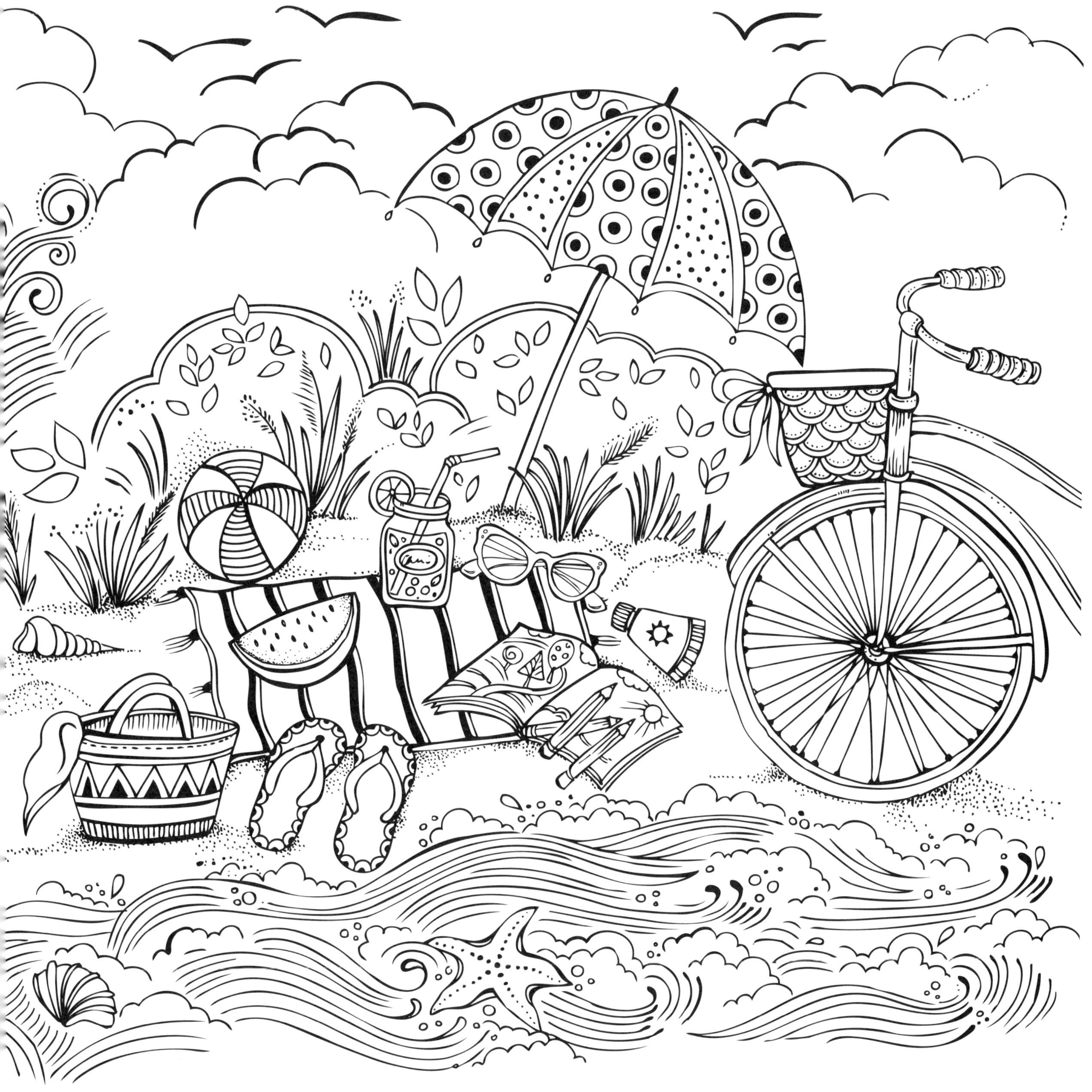

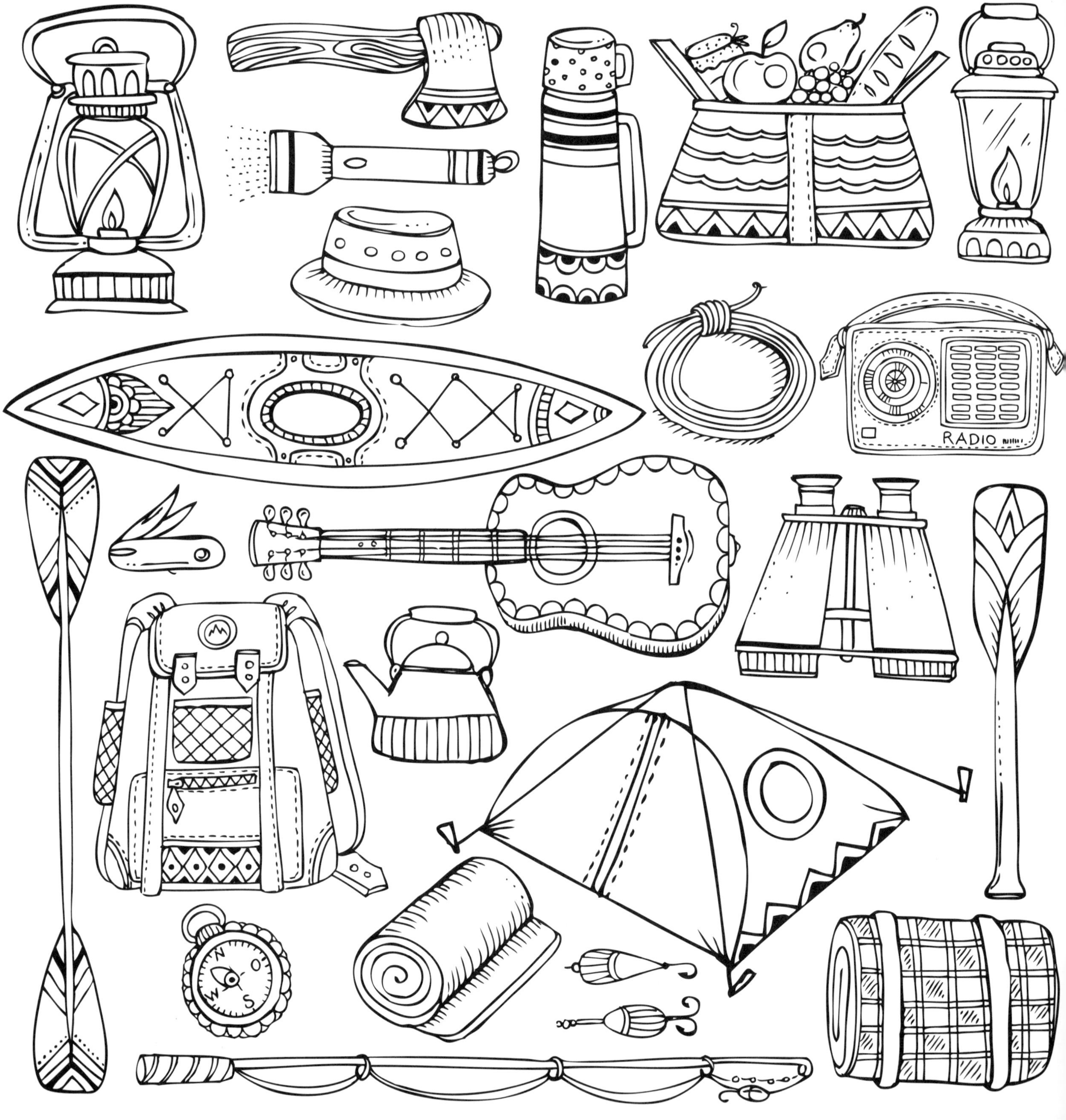
RADIO

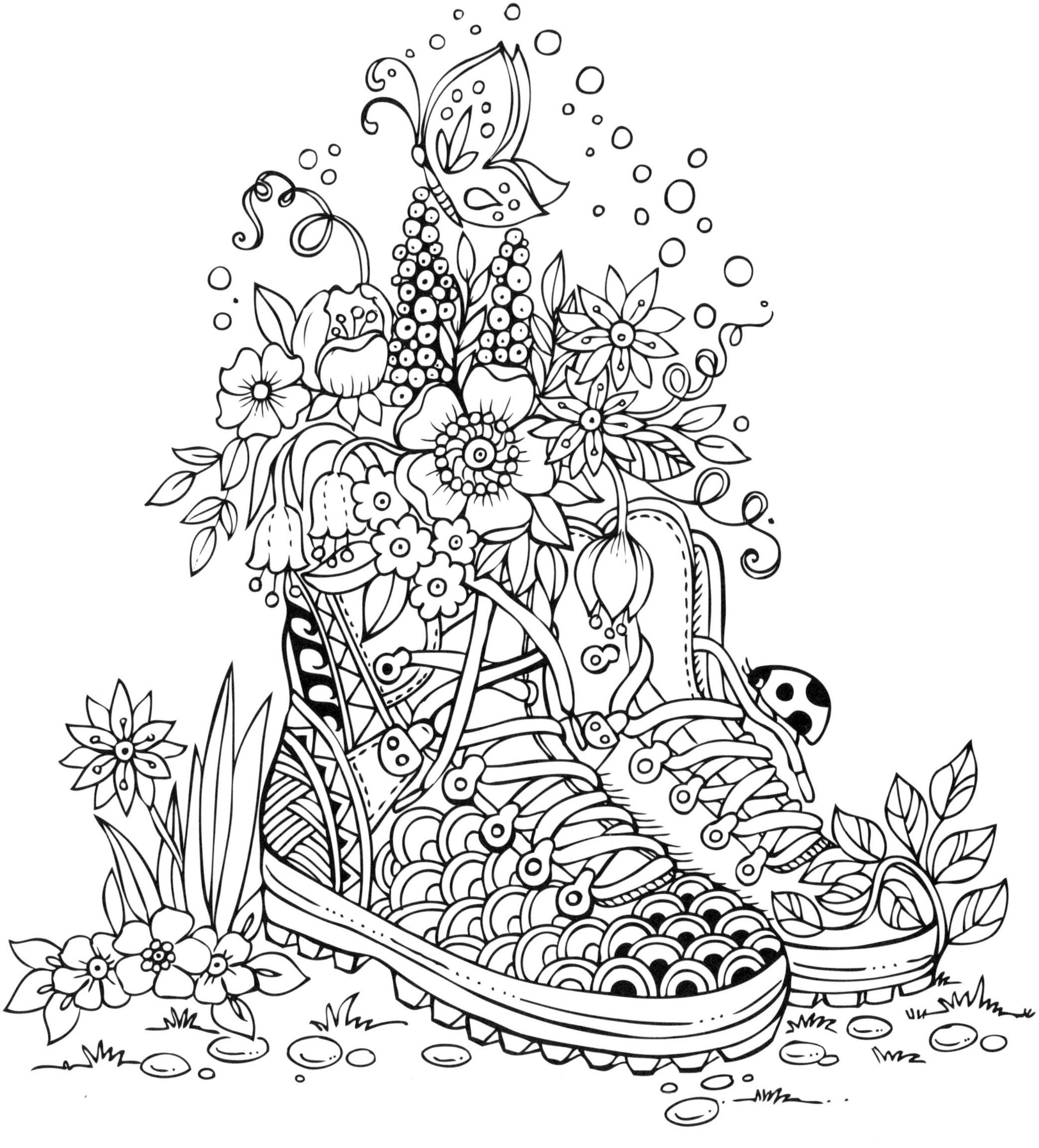

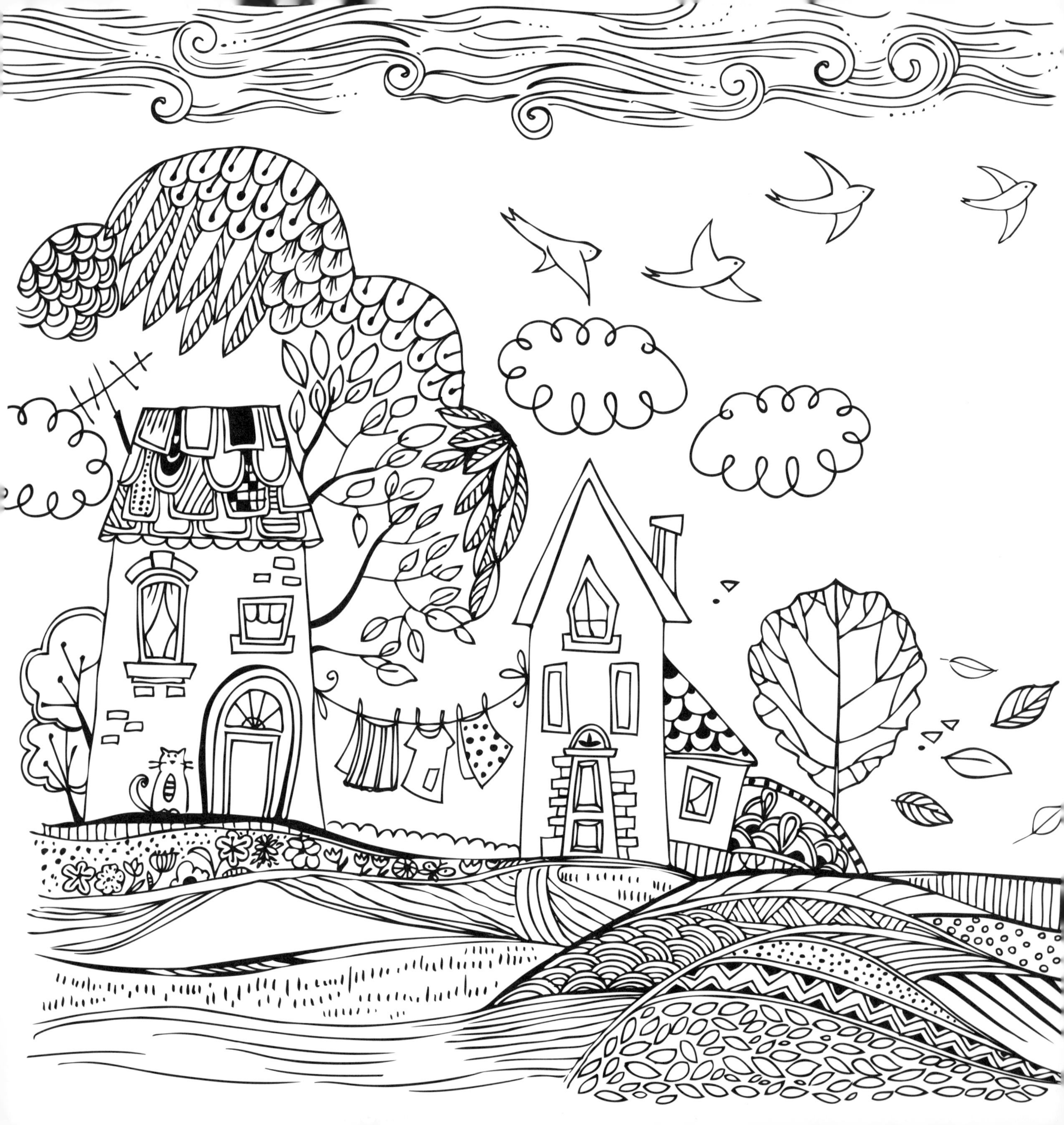

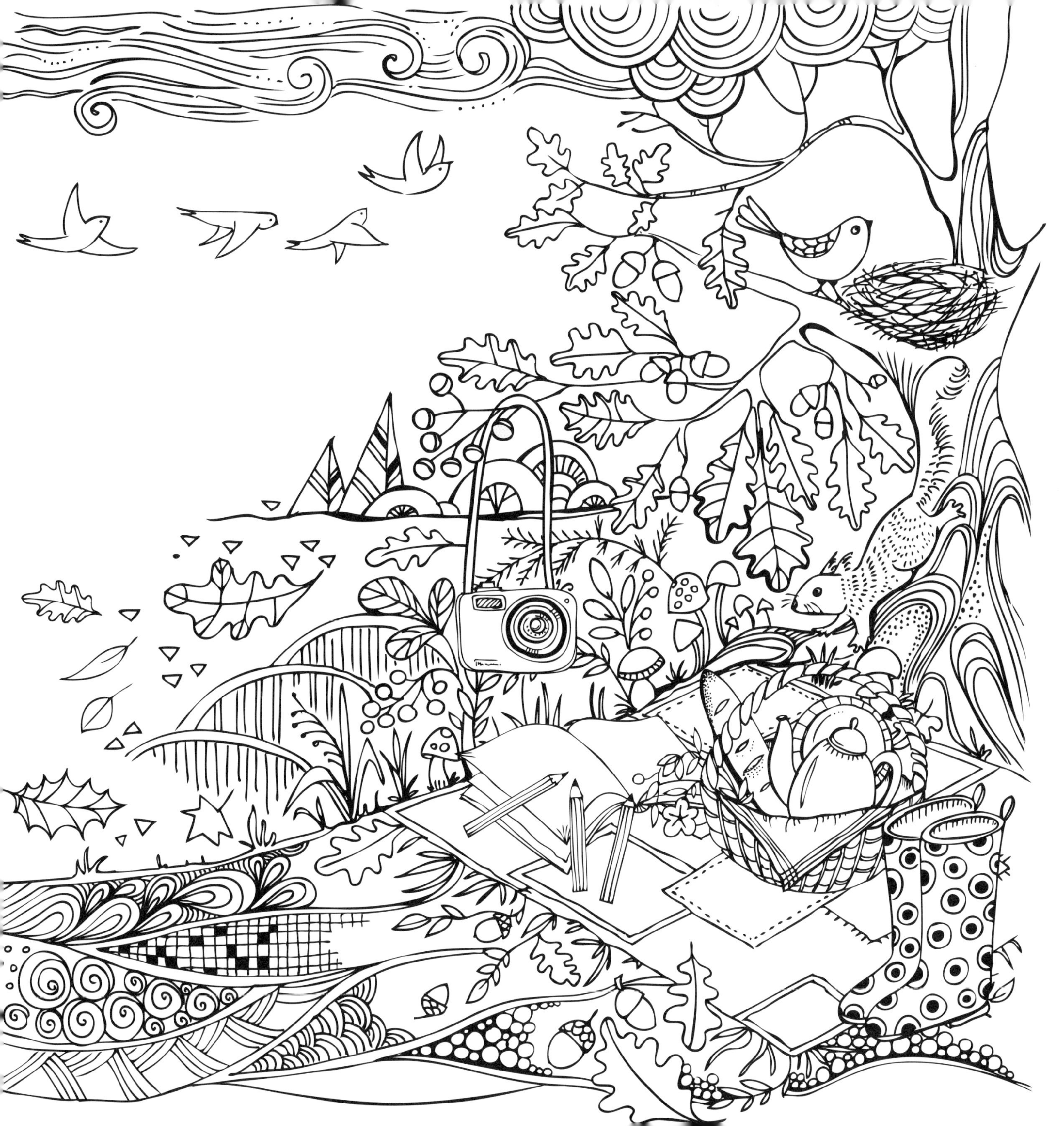

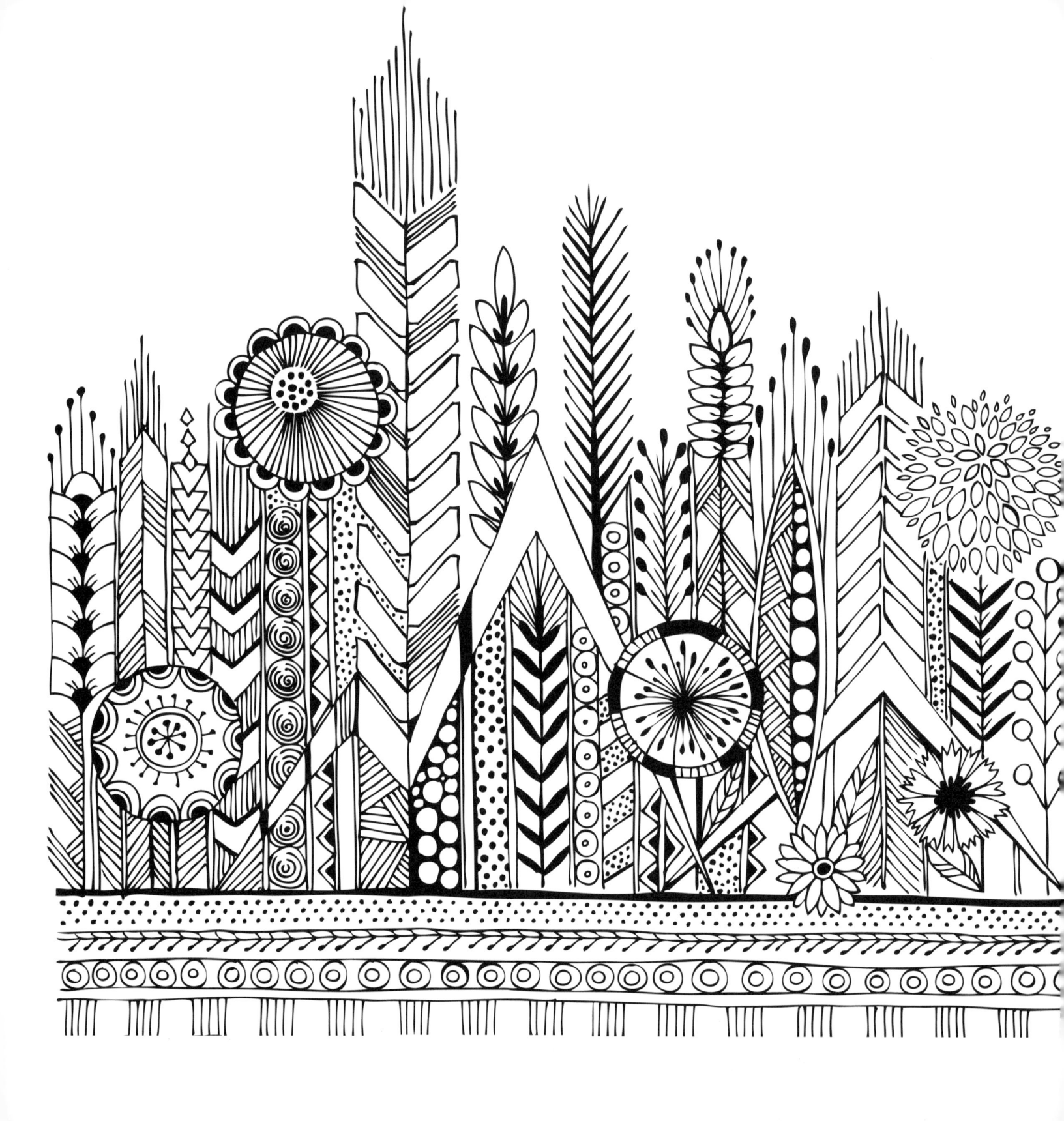

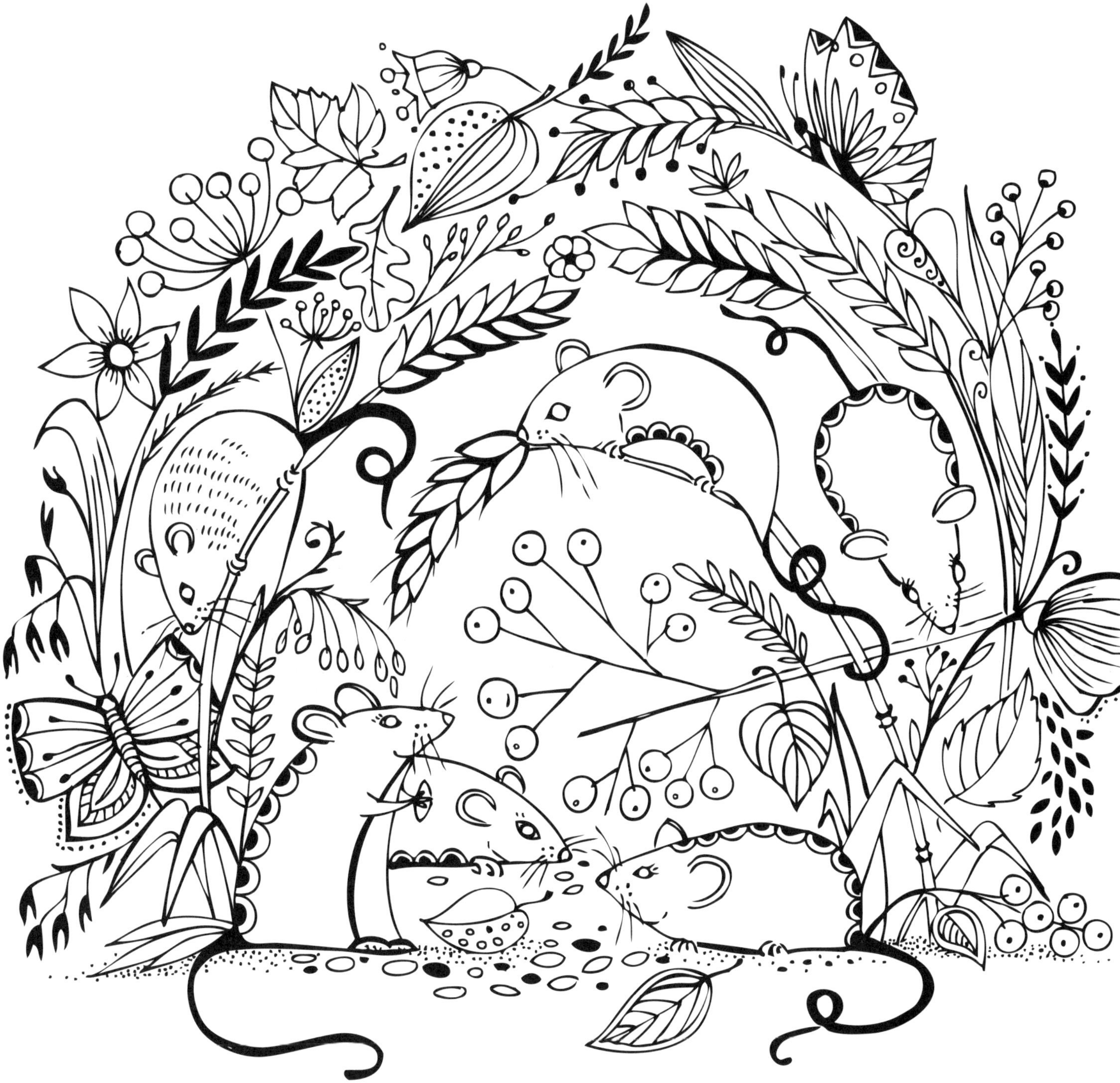

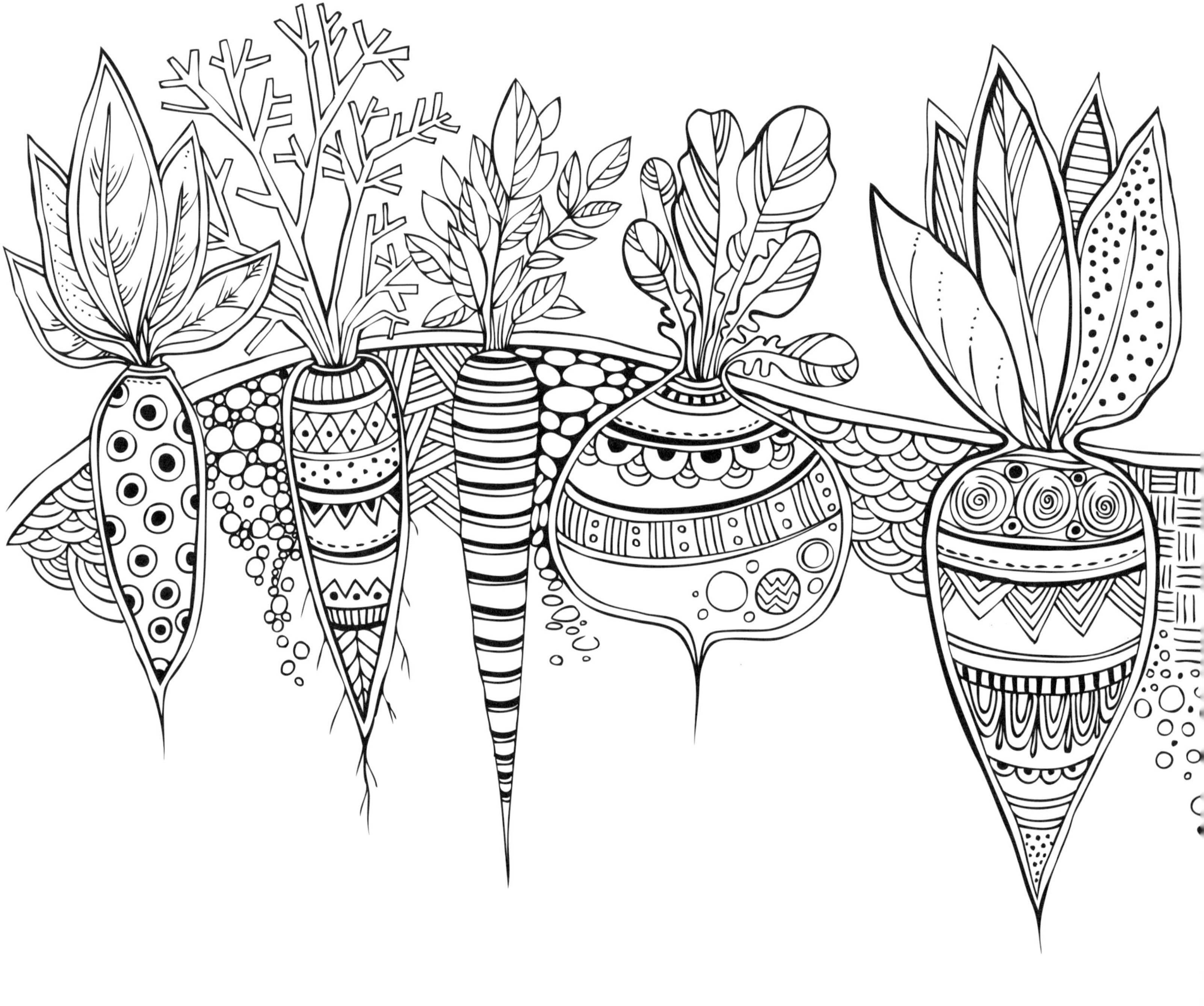

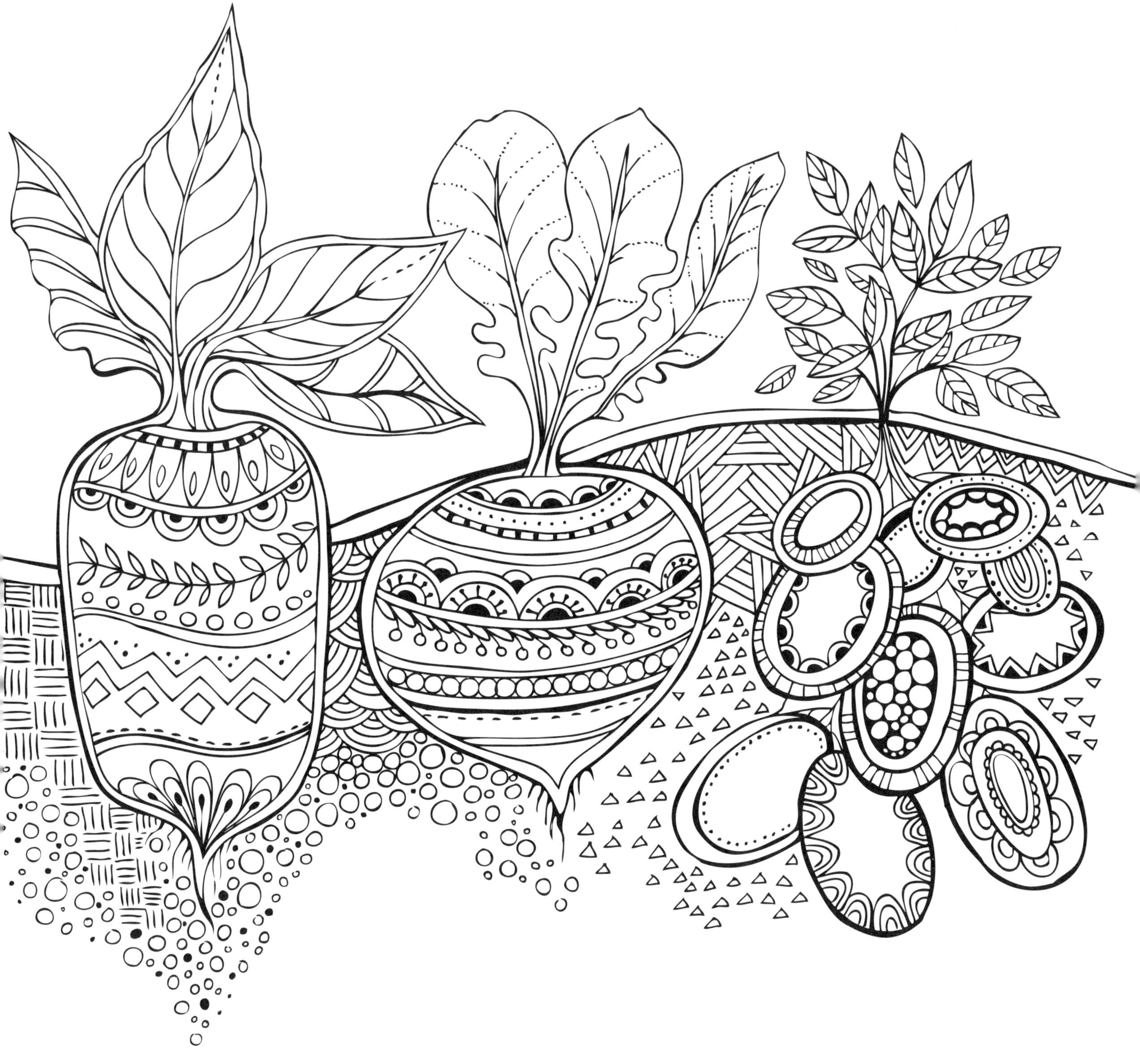

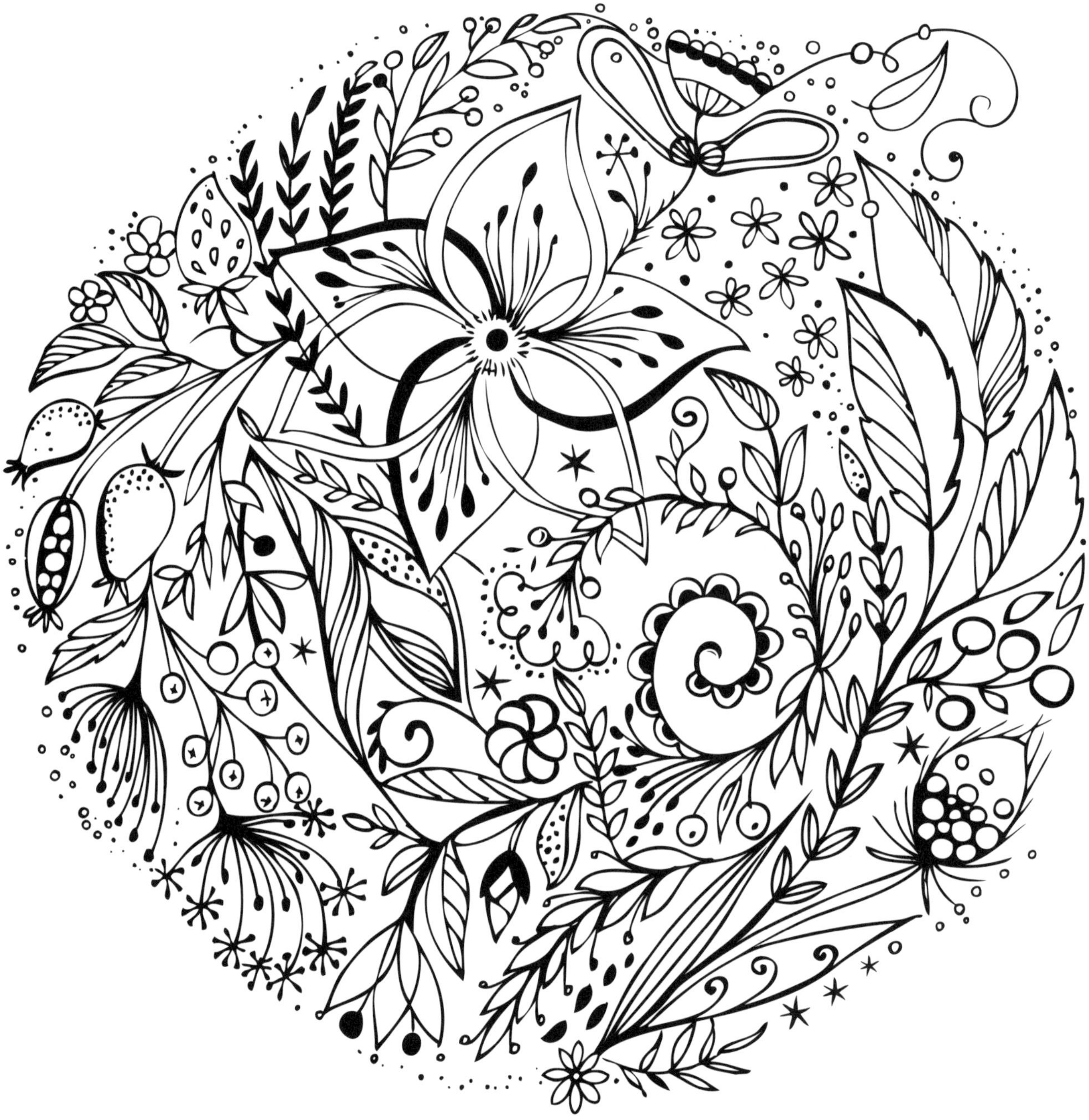

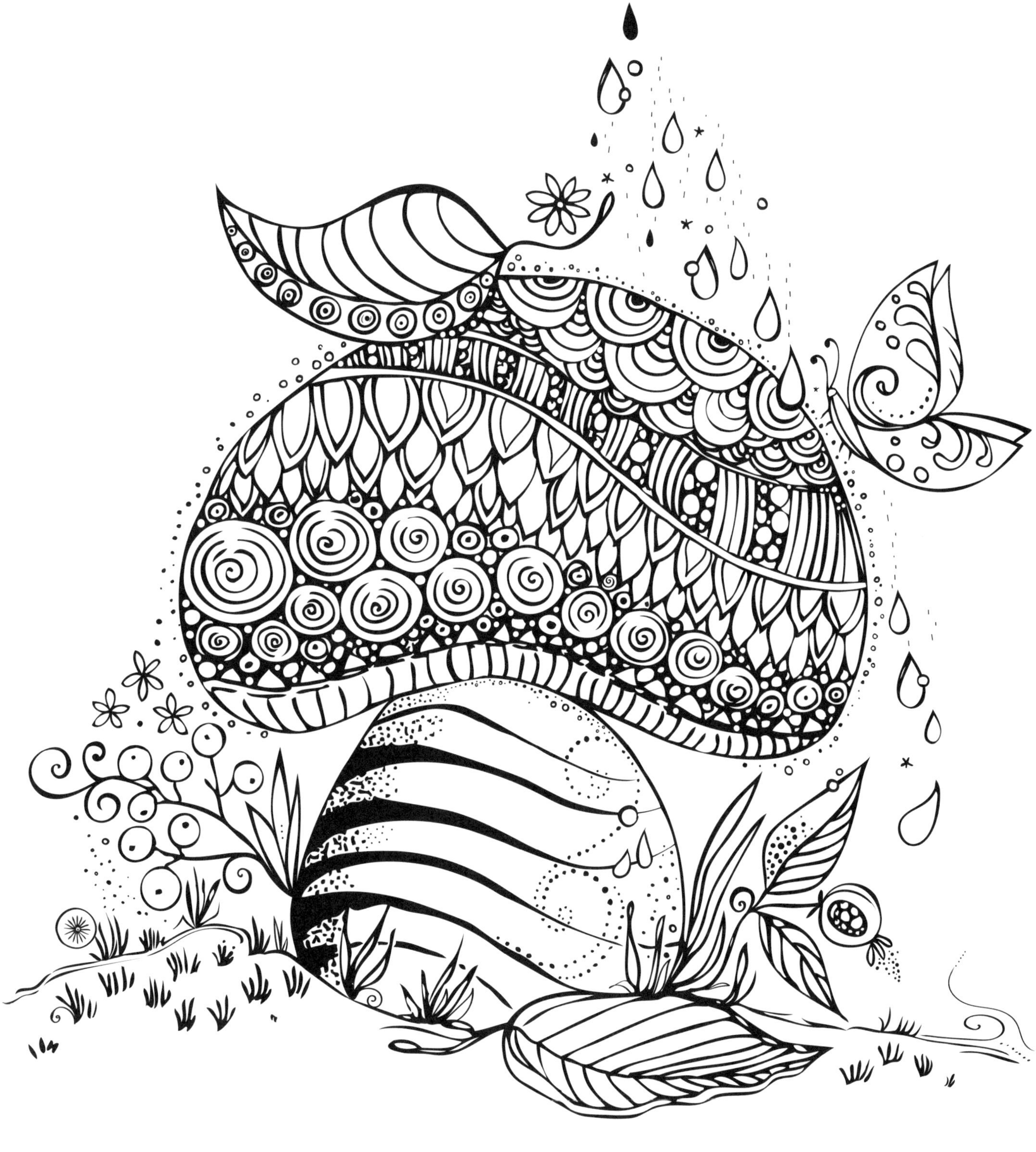

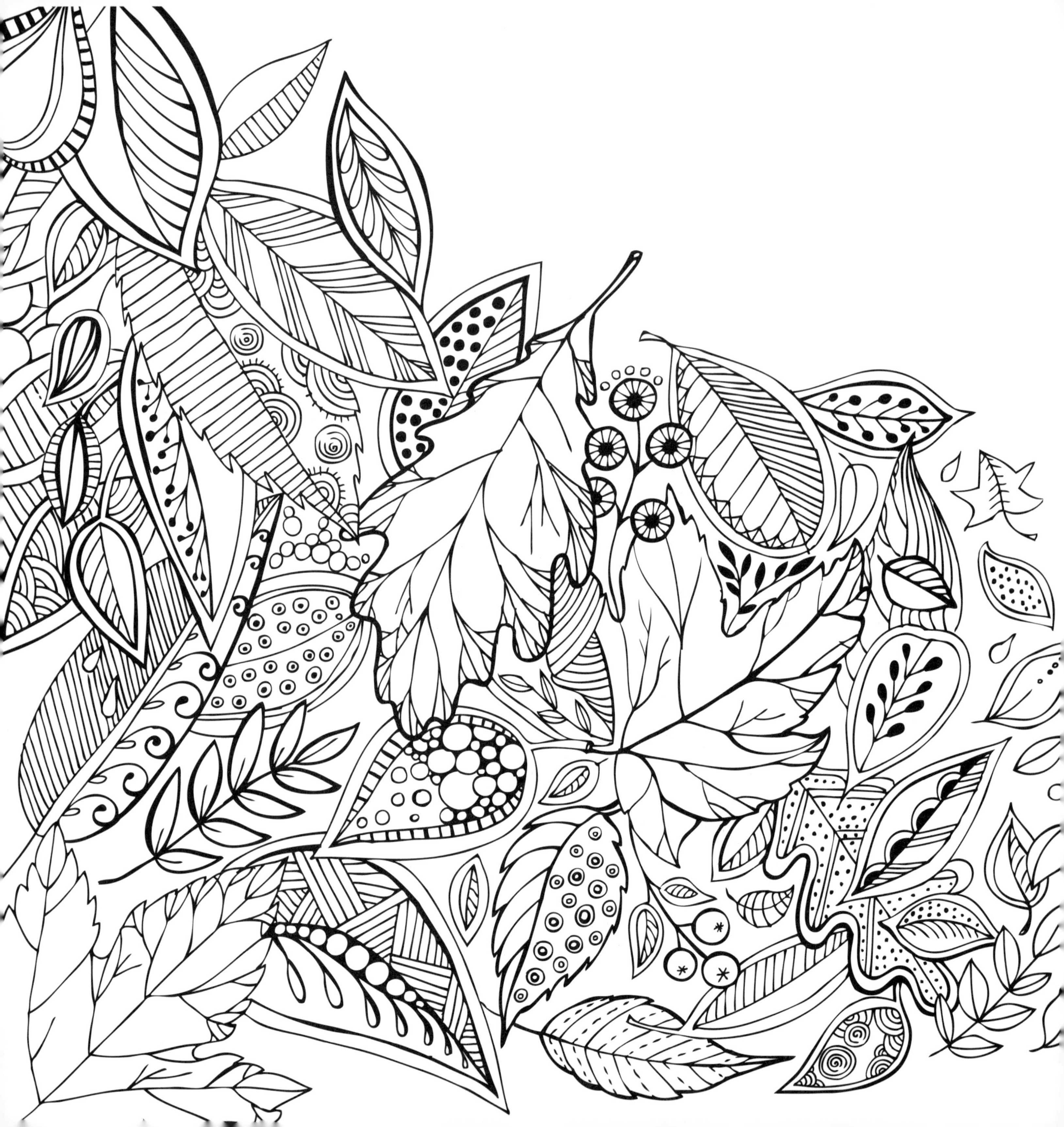

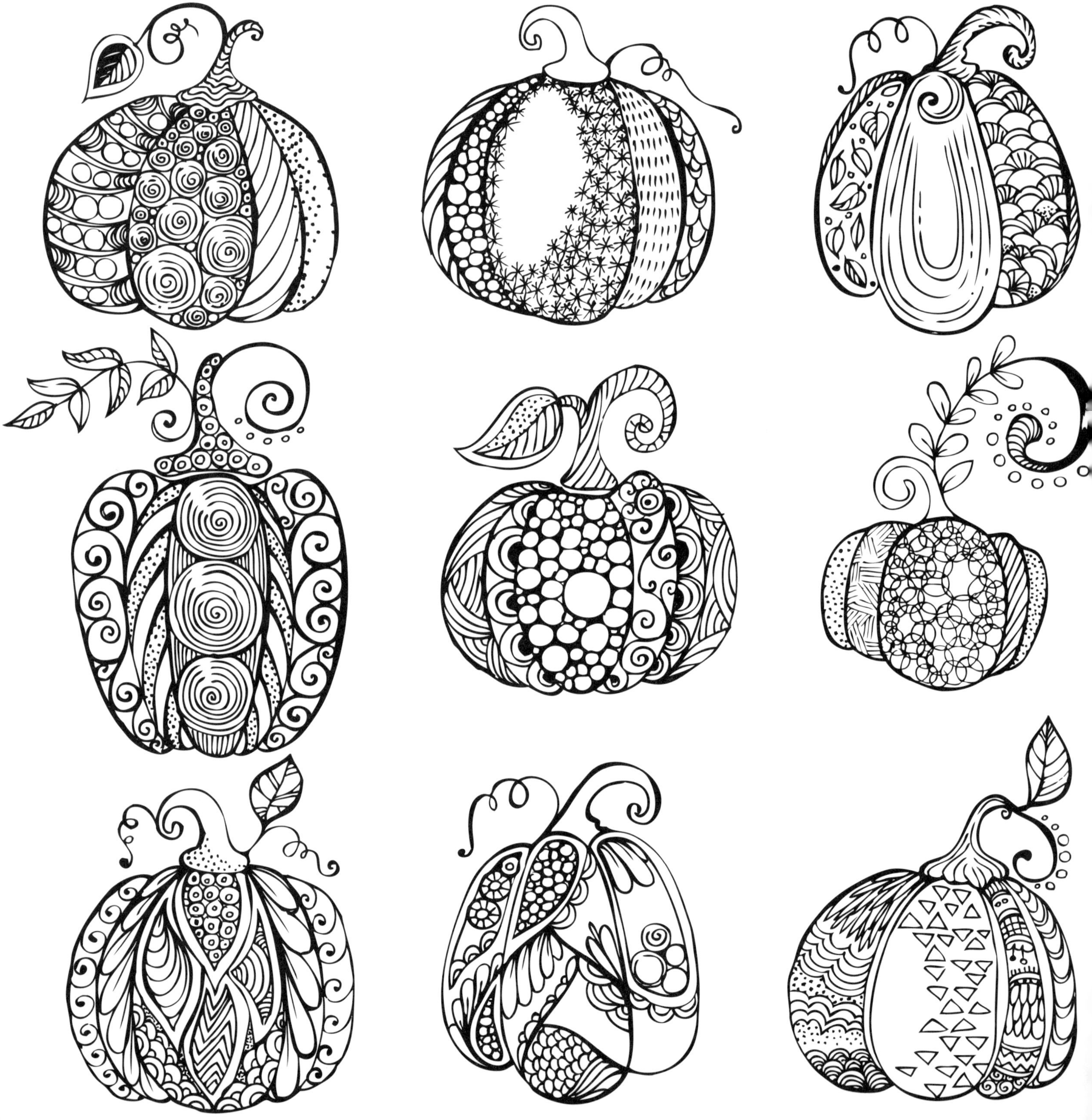

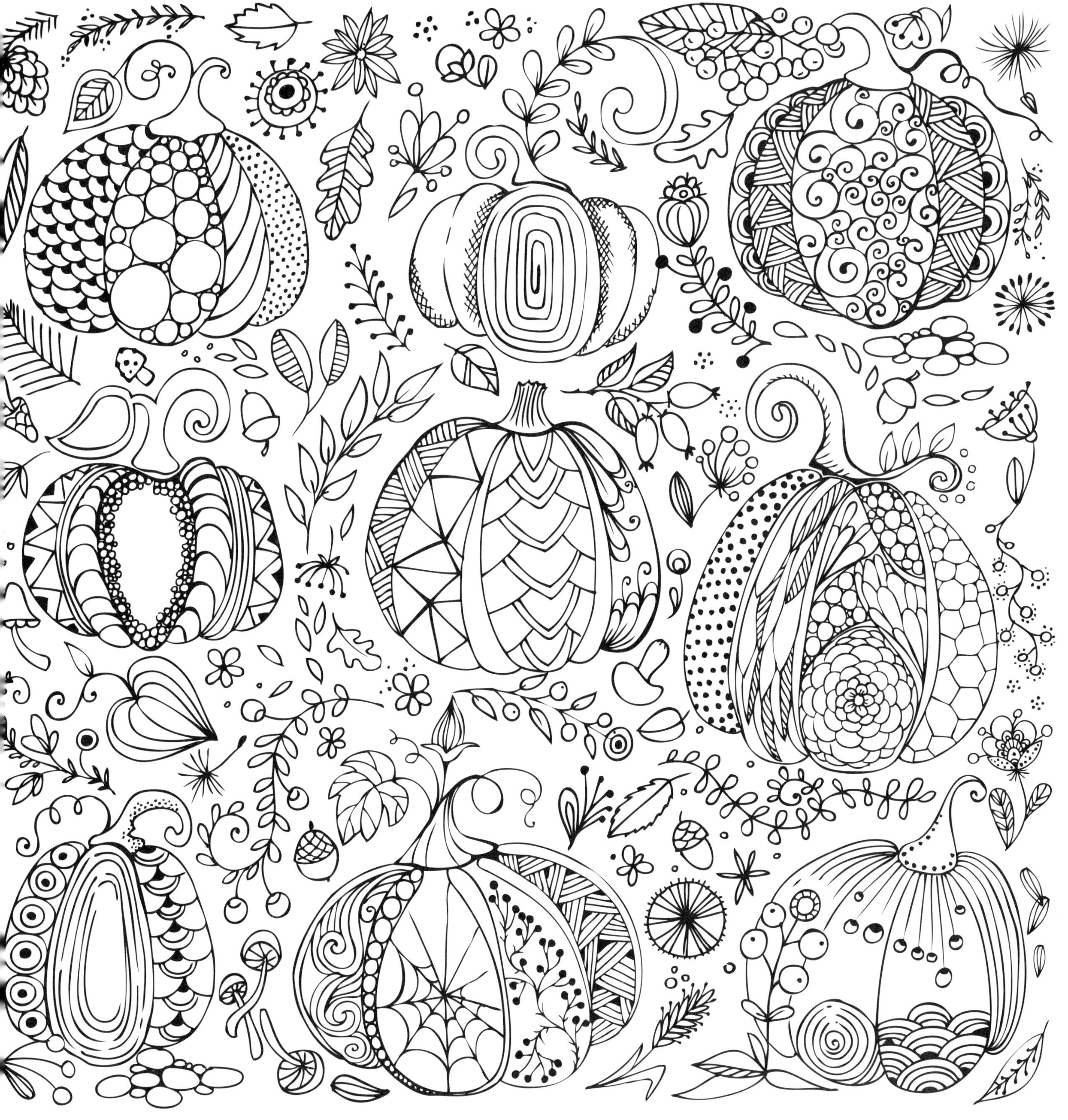

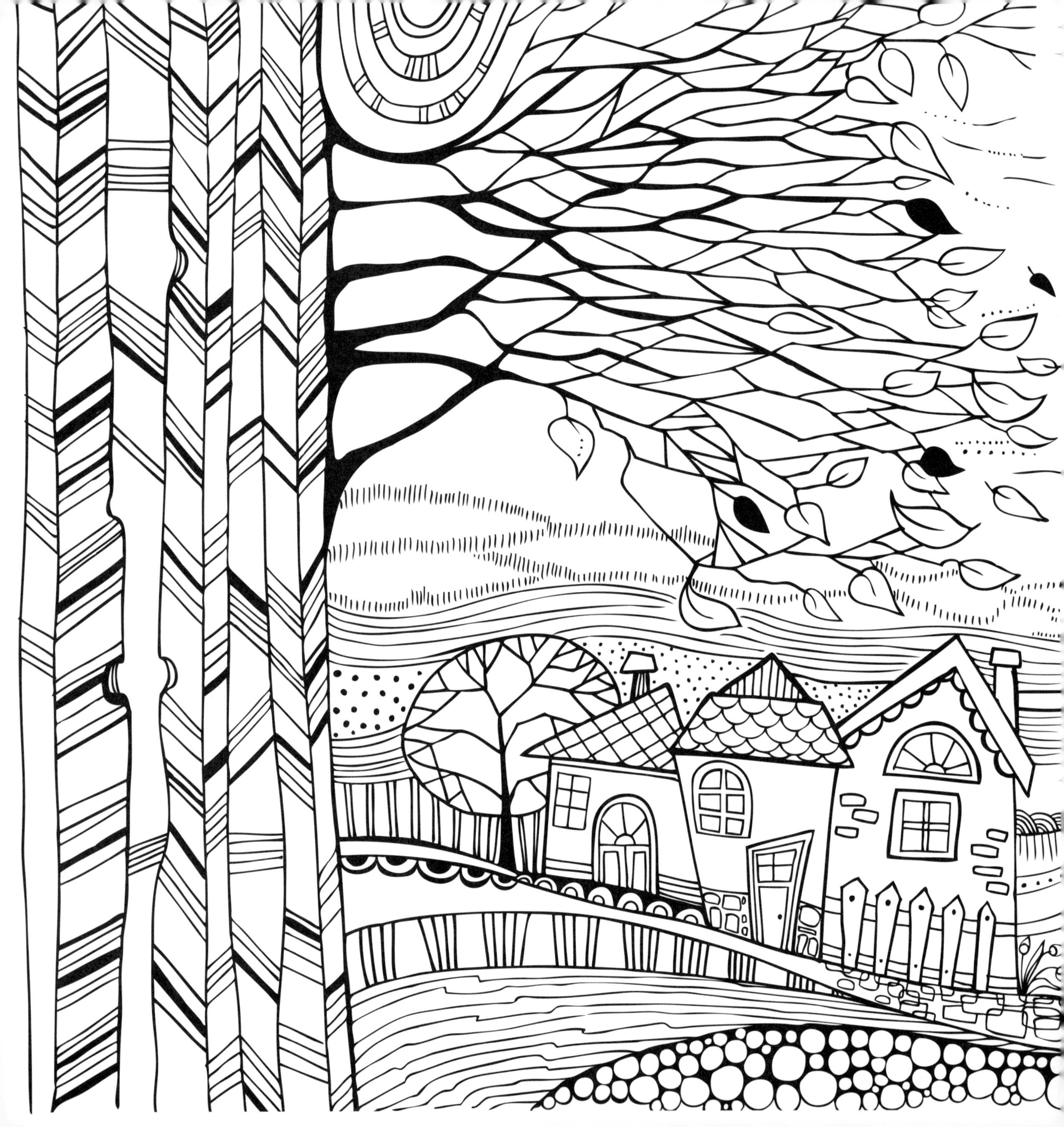

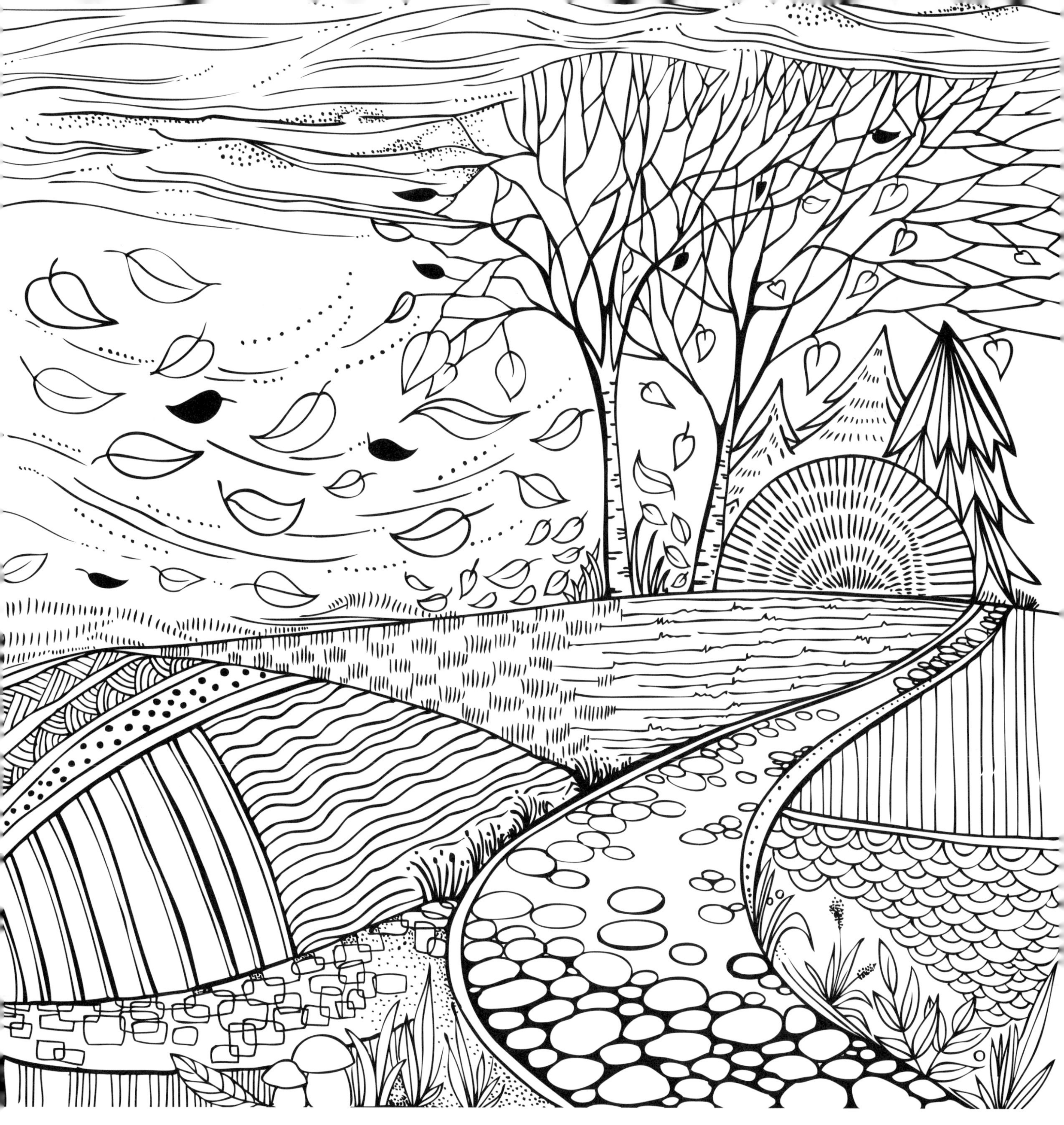

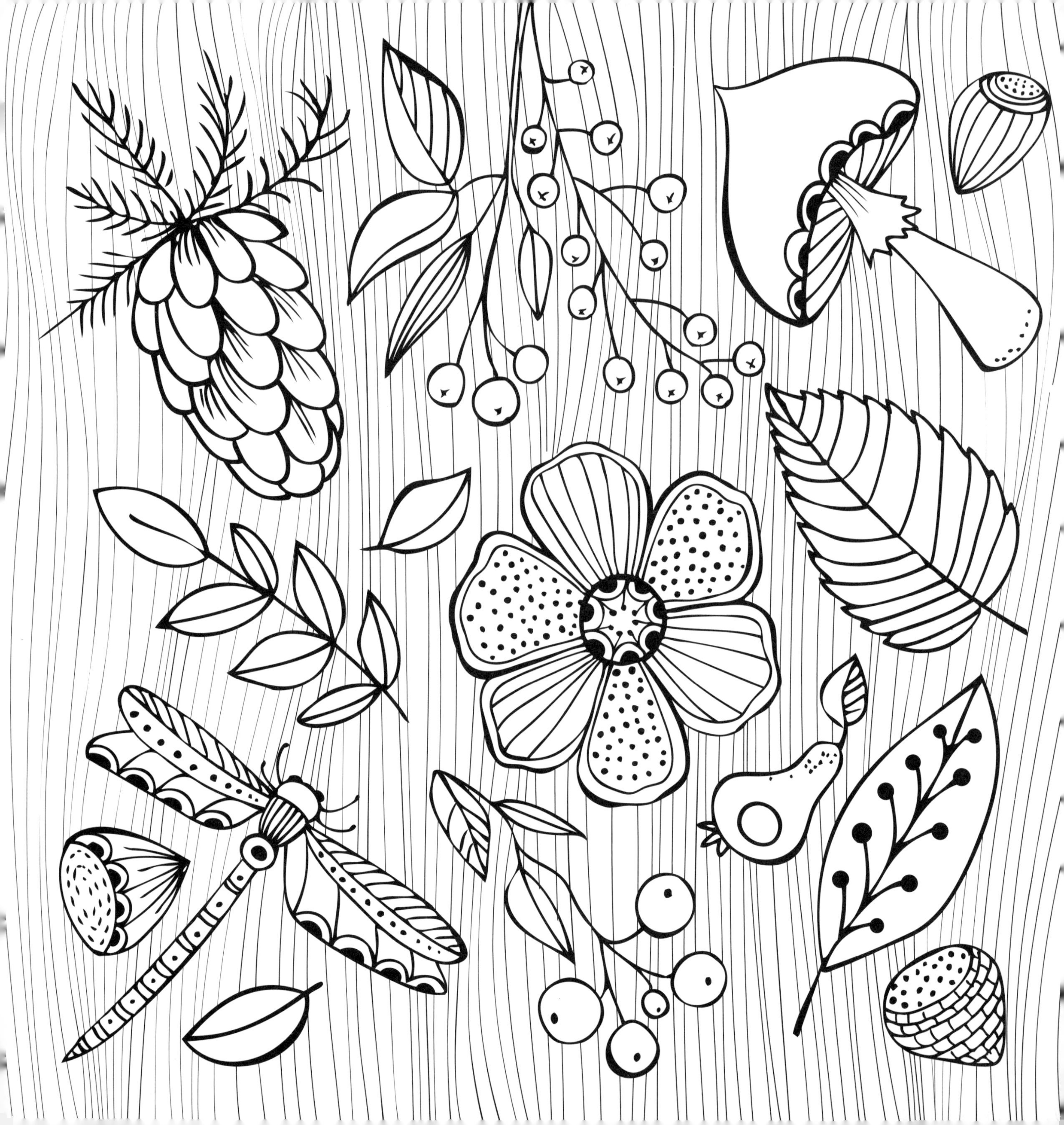

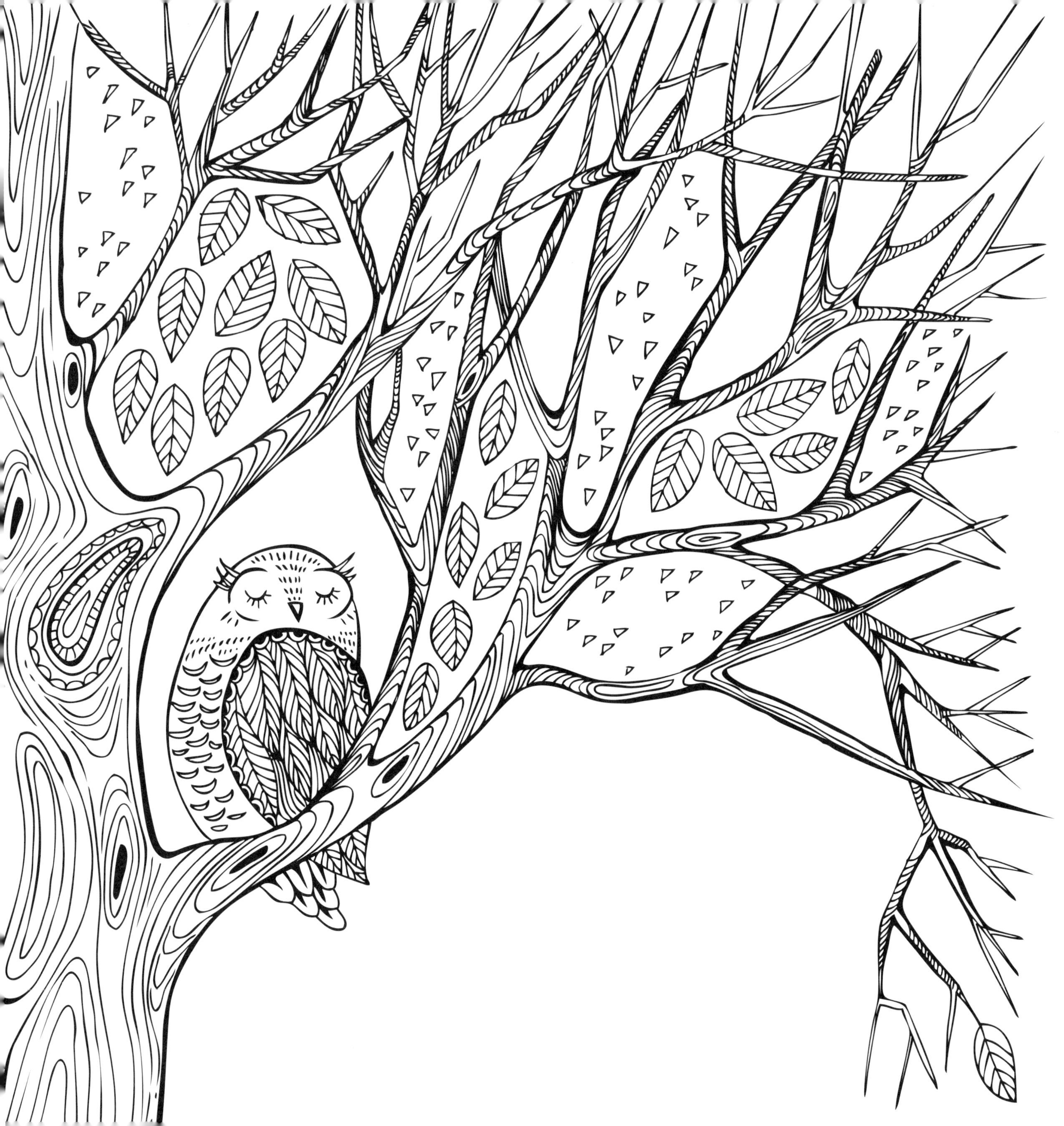

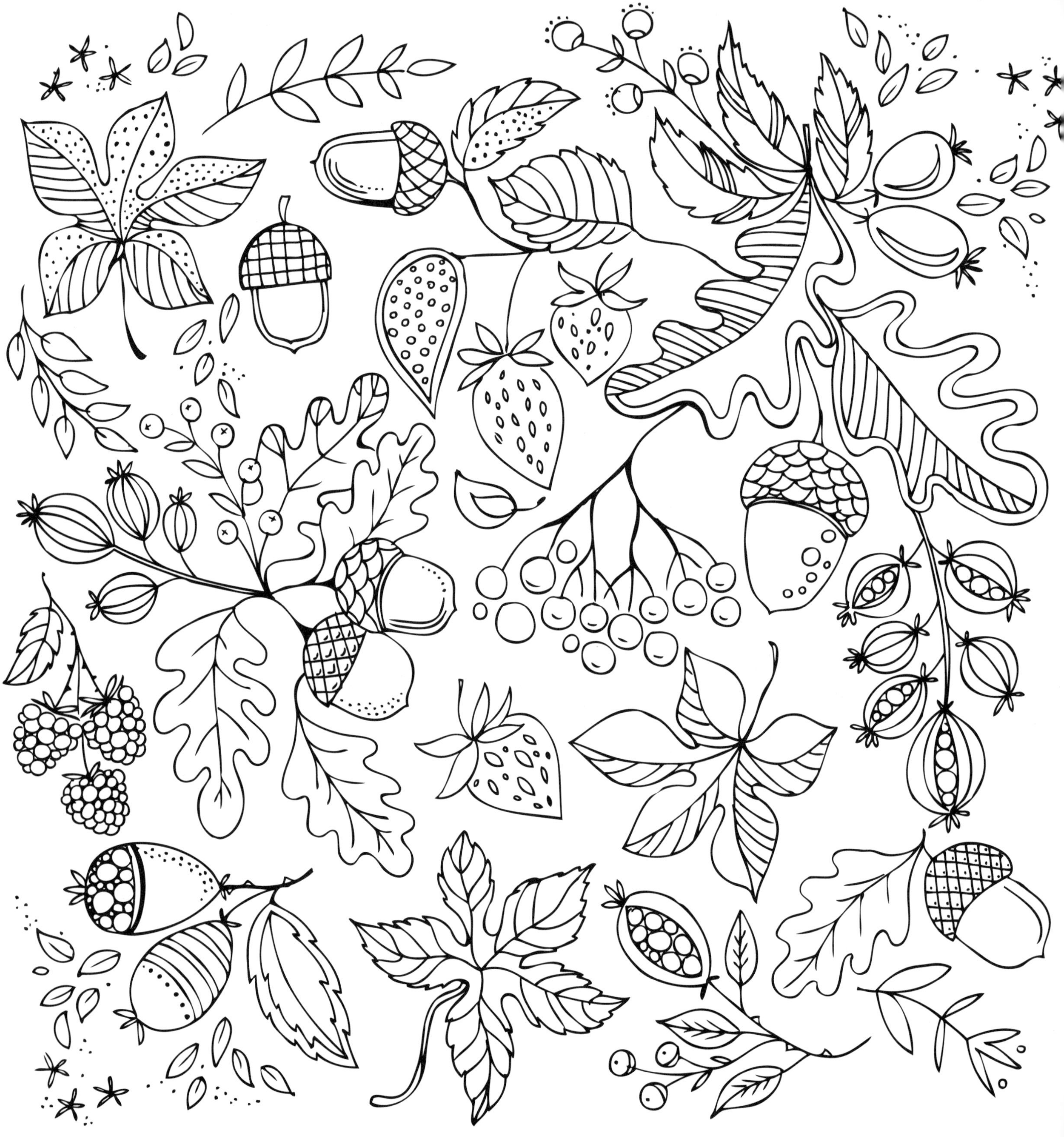

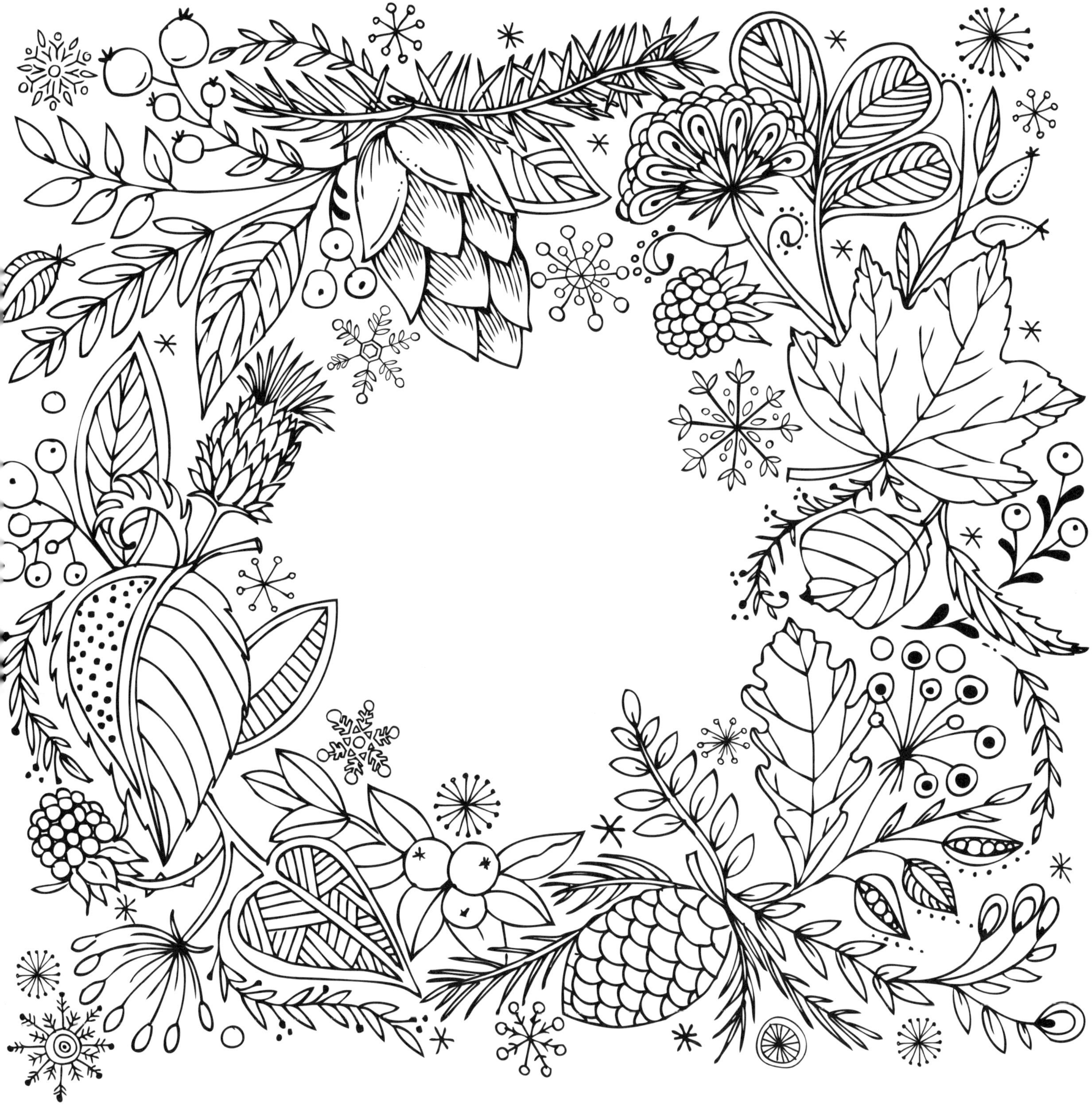

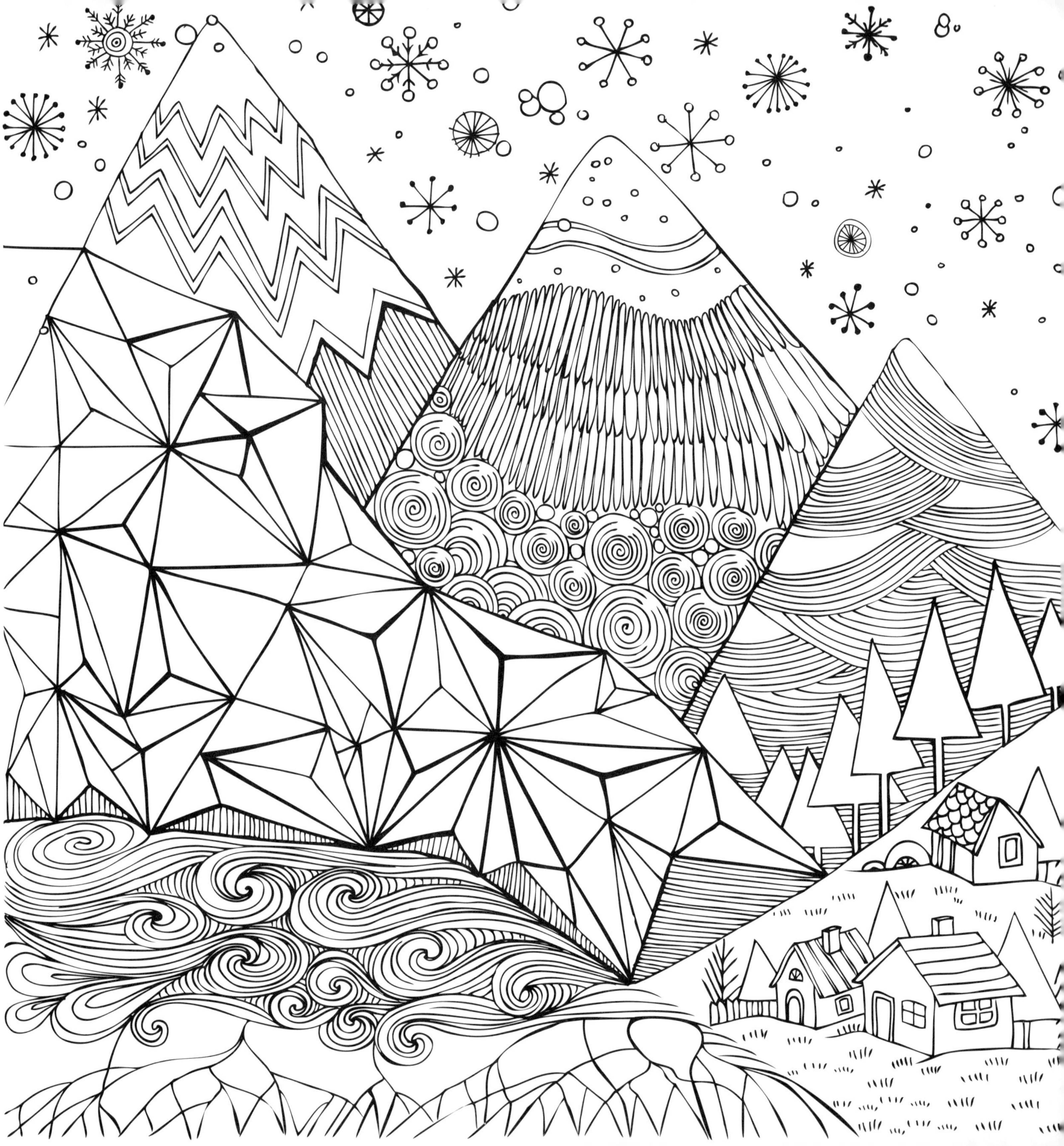

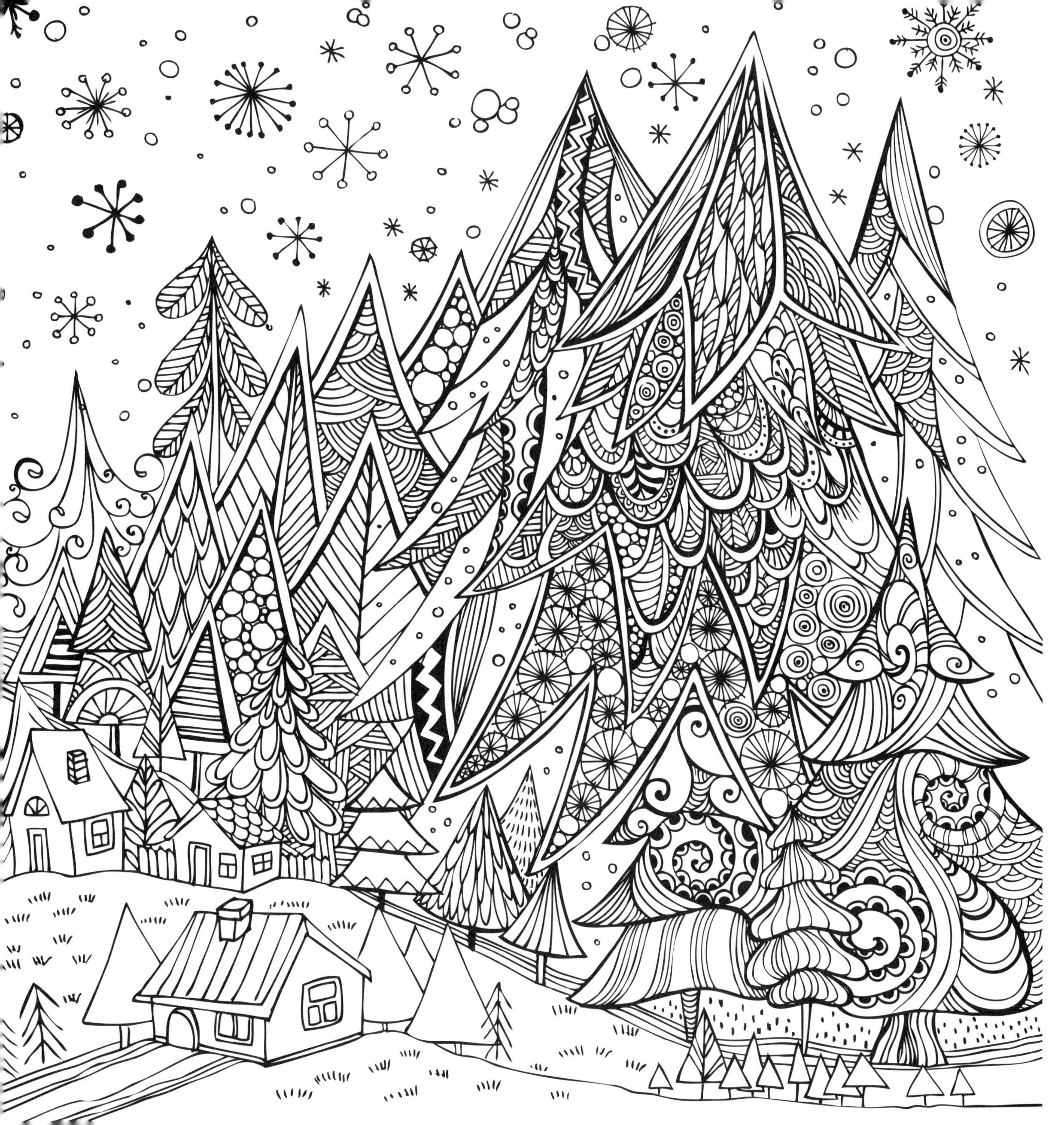

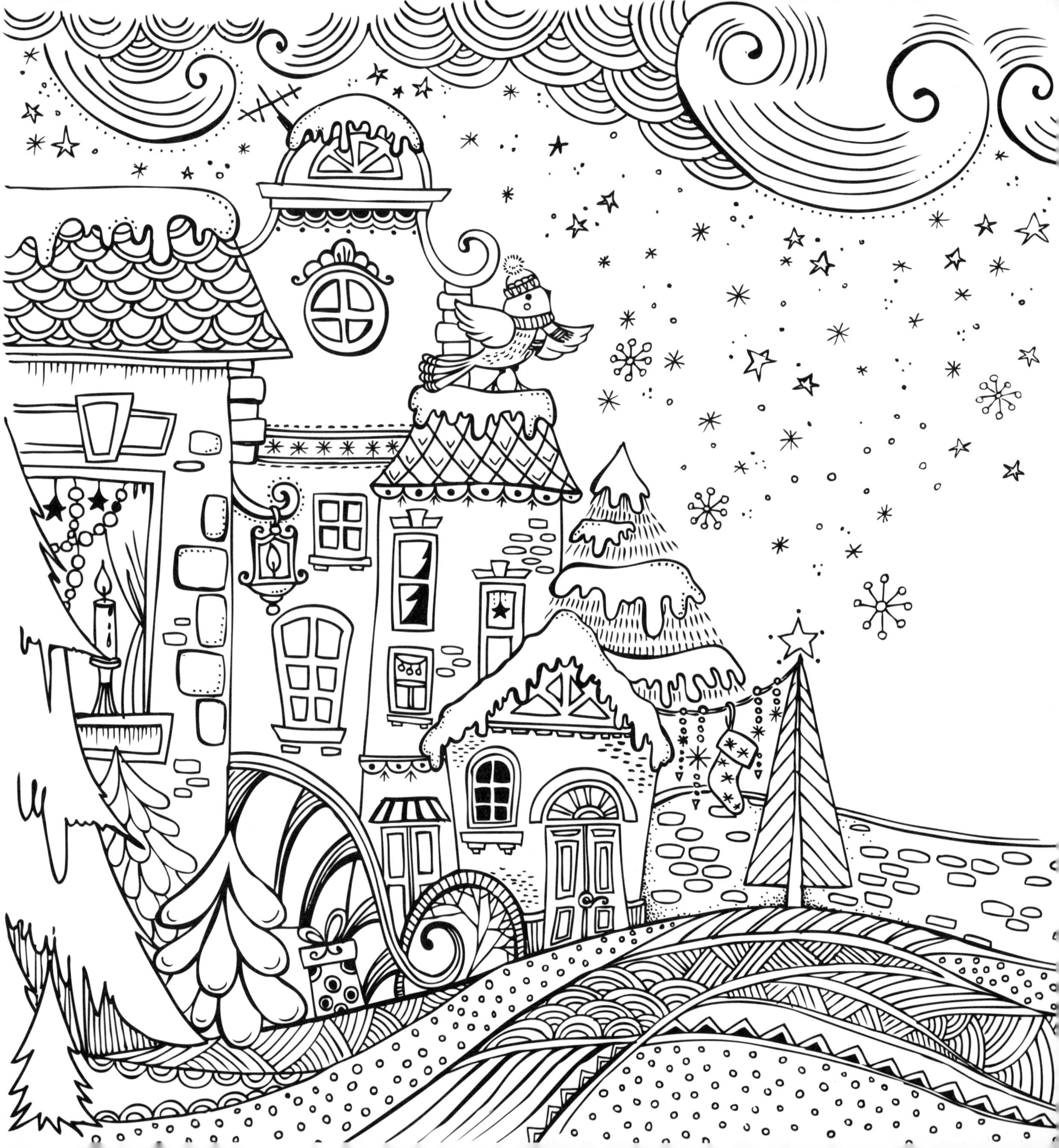

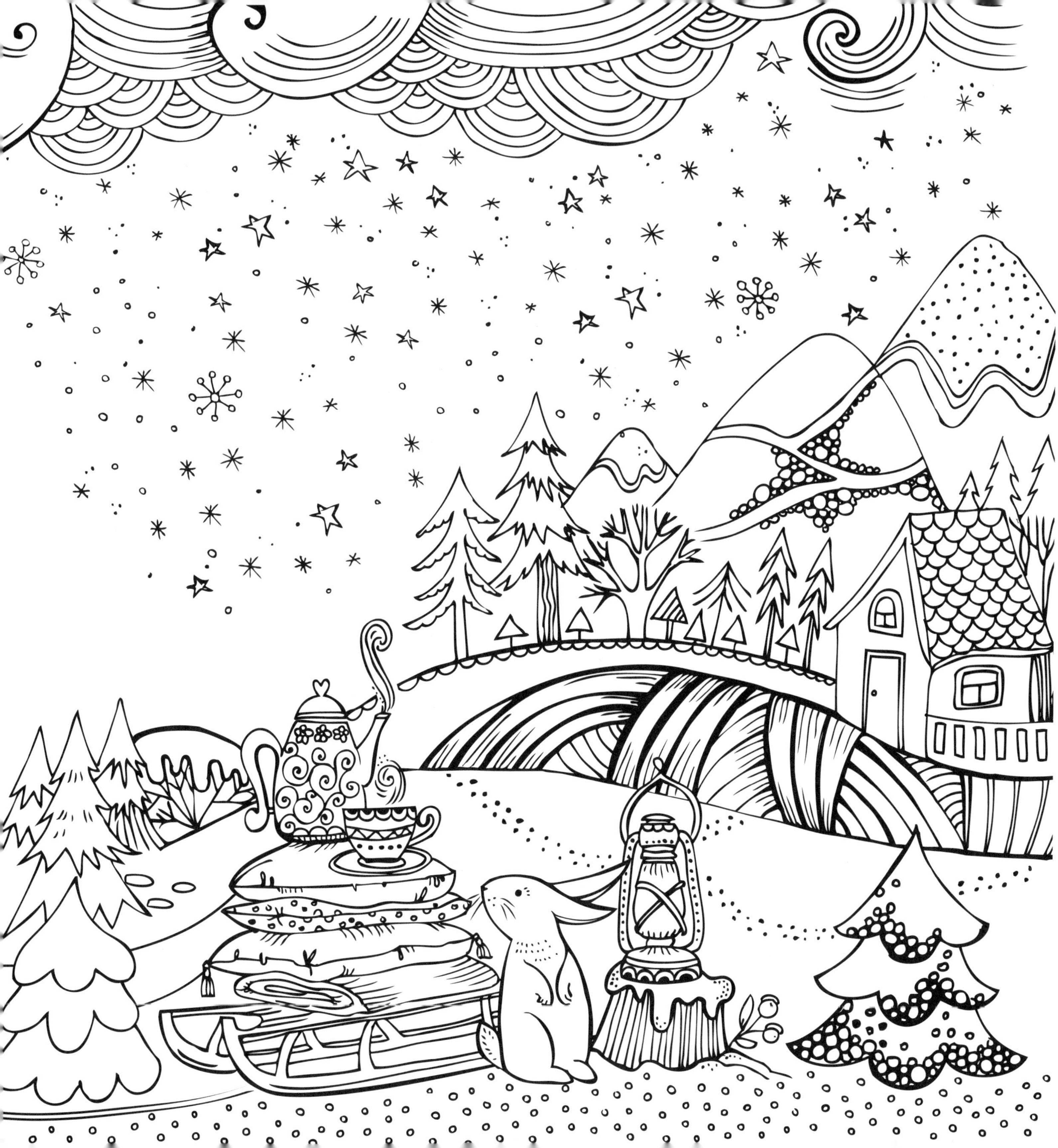

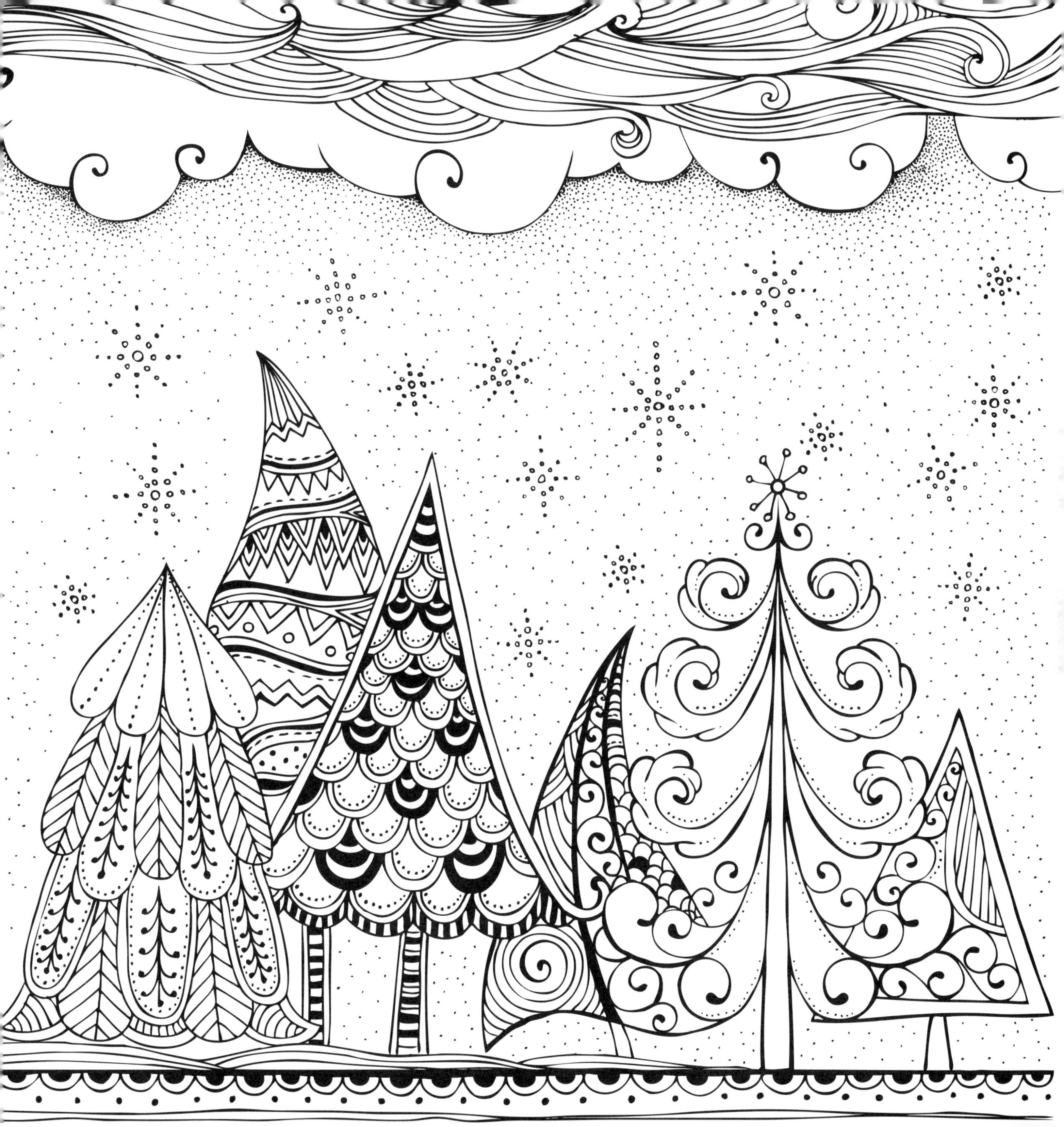

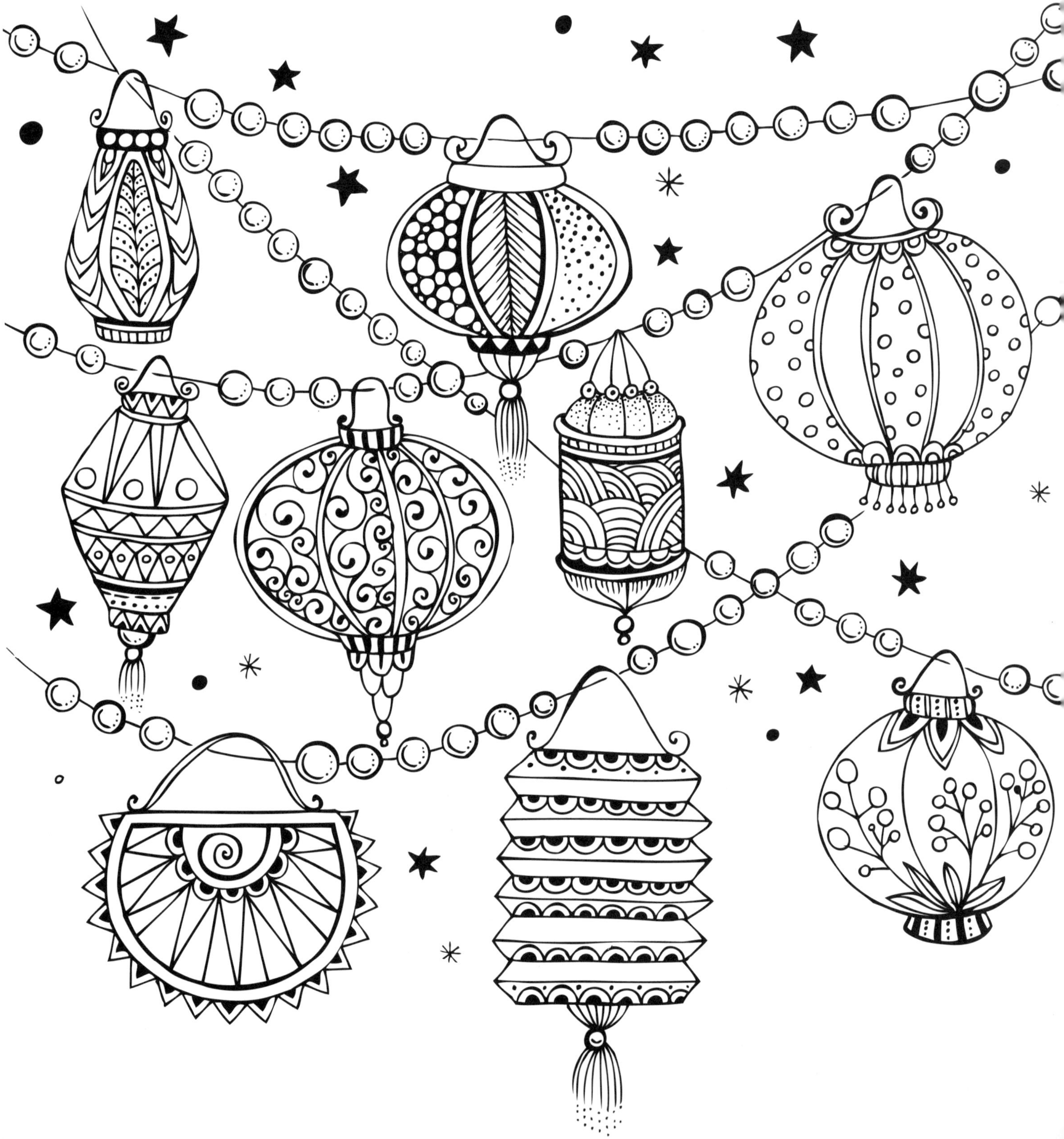

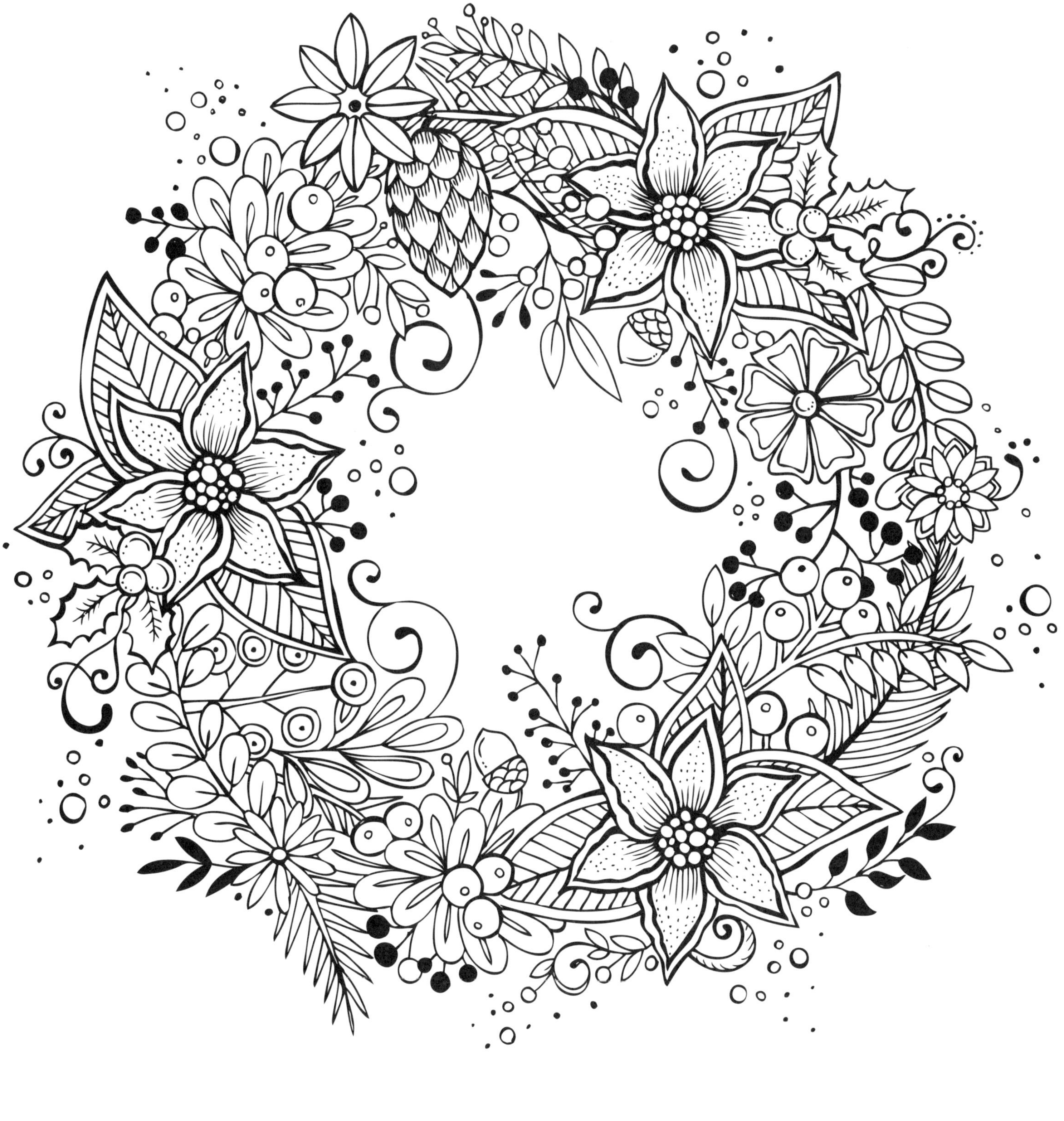

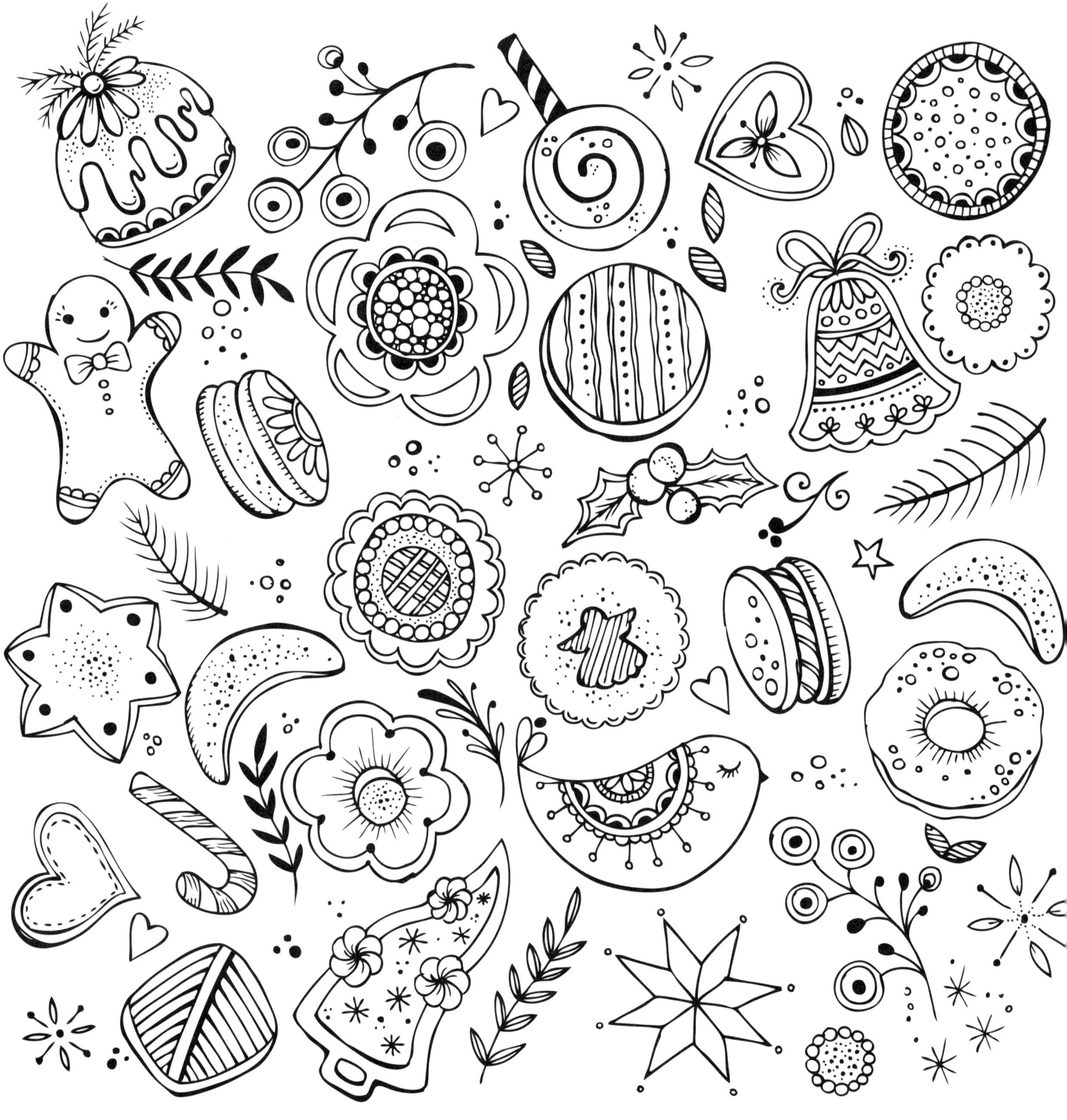

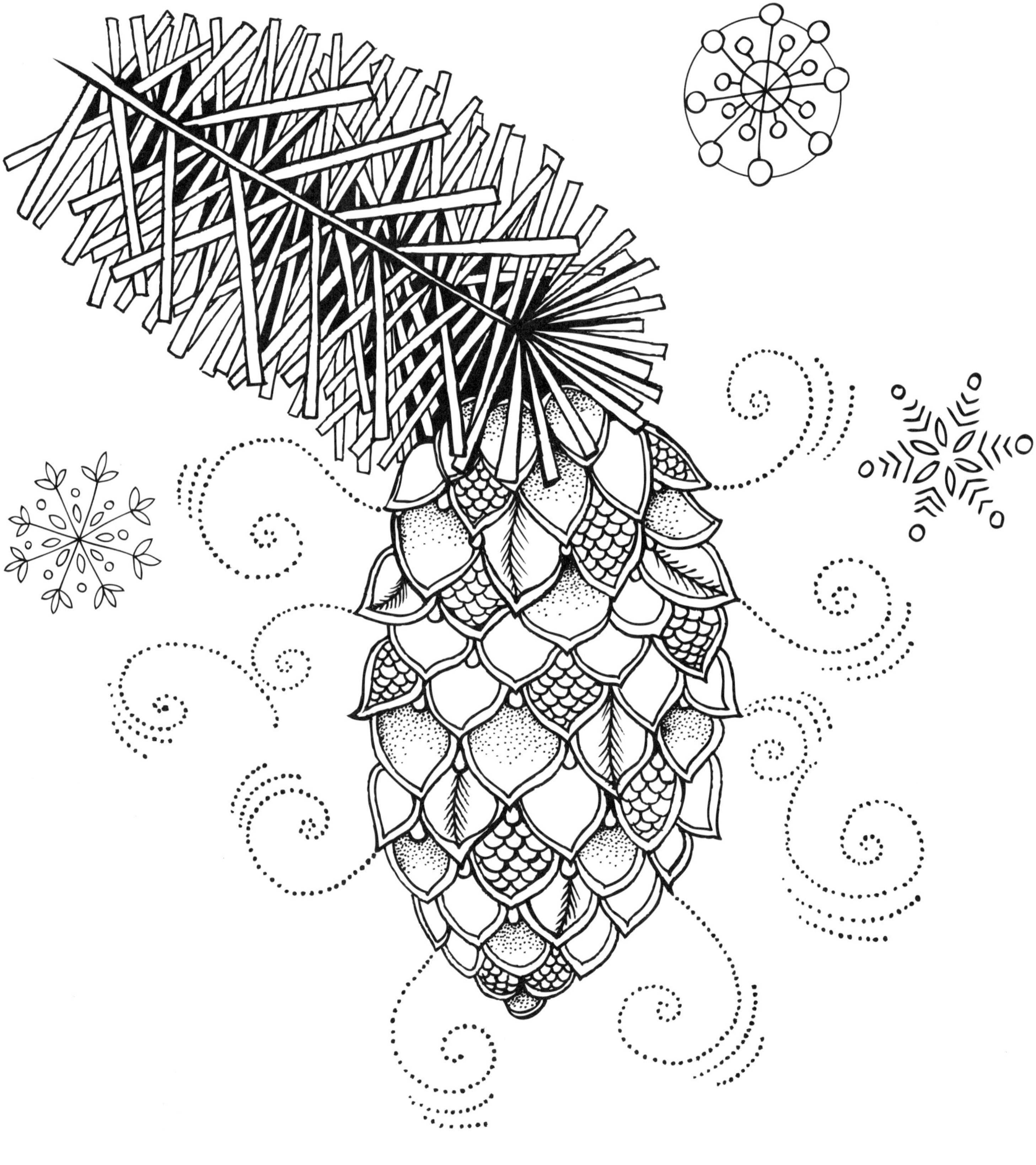

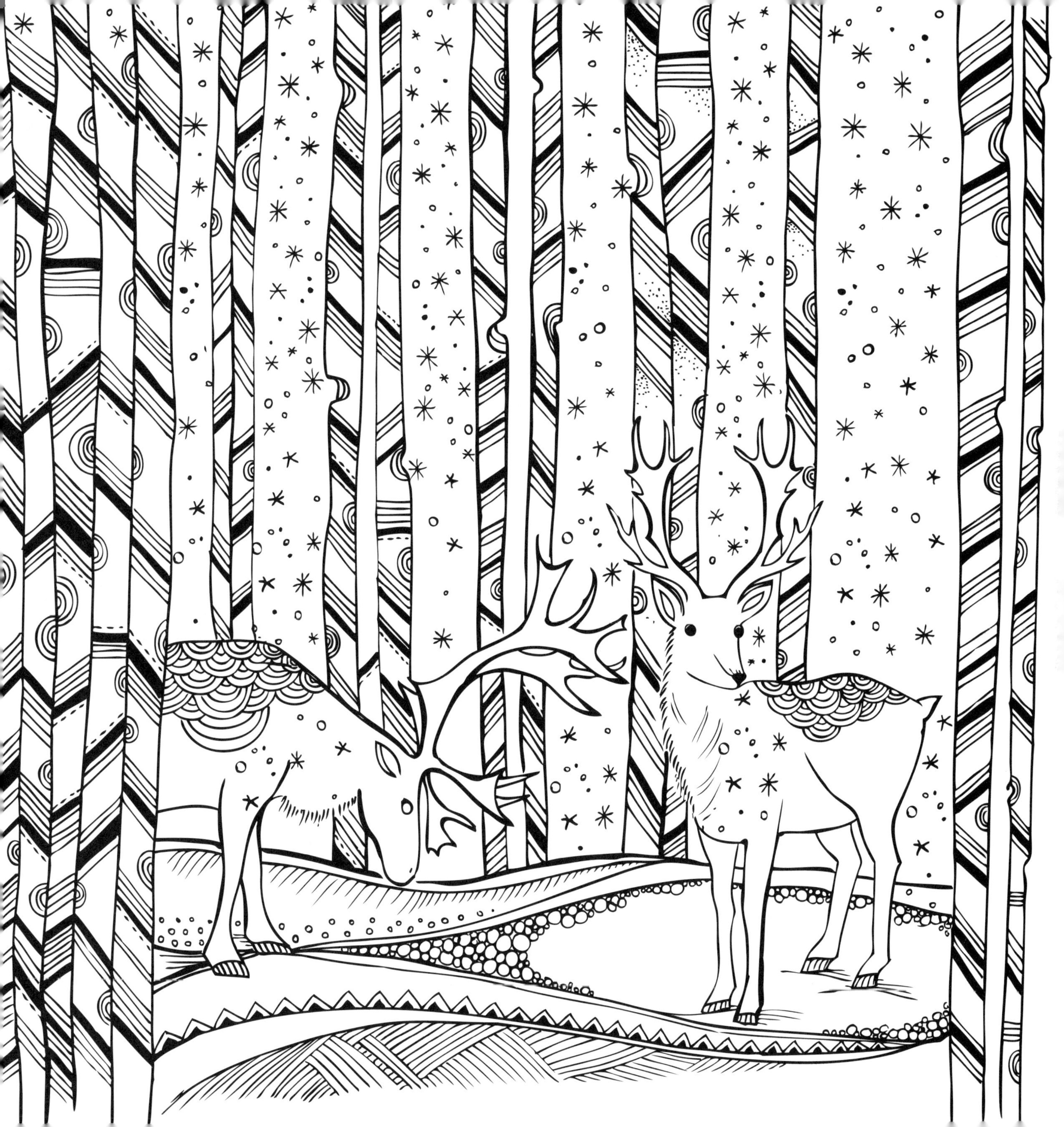

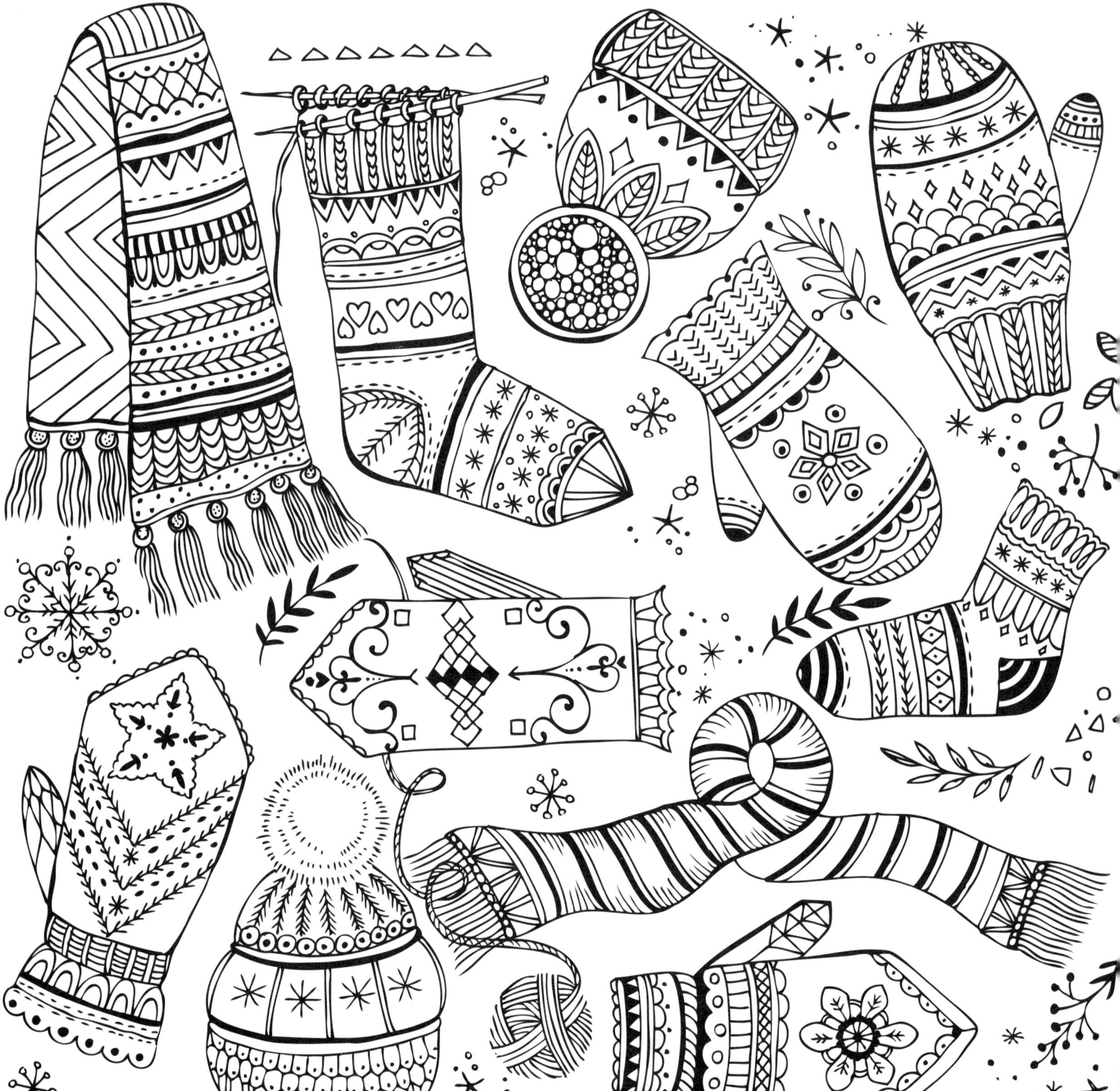

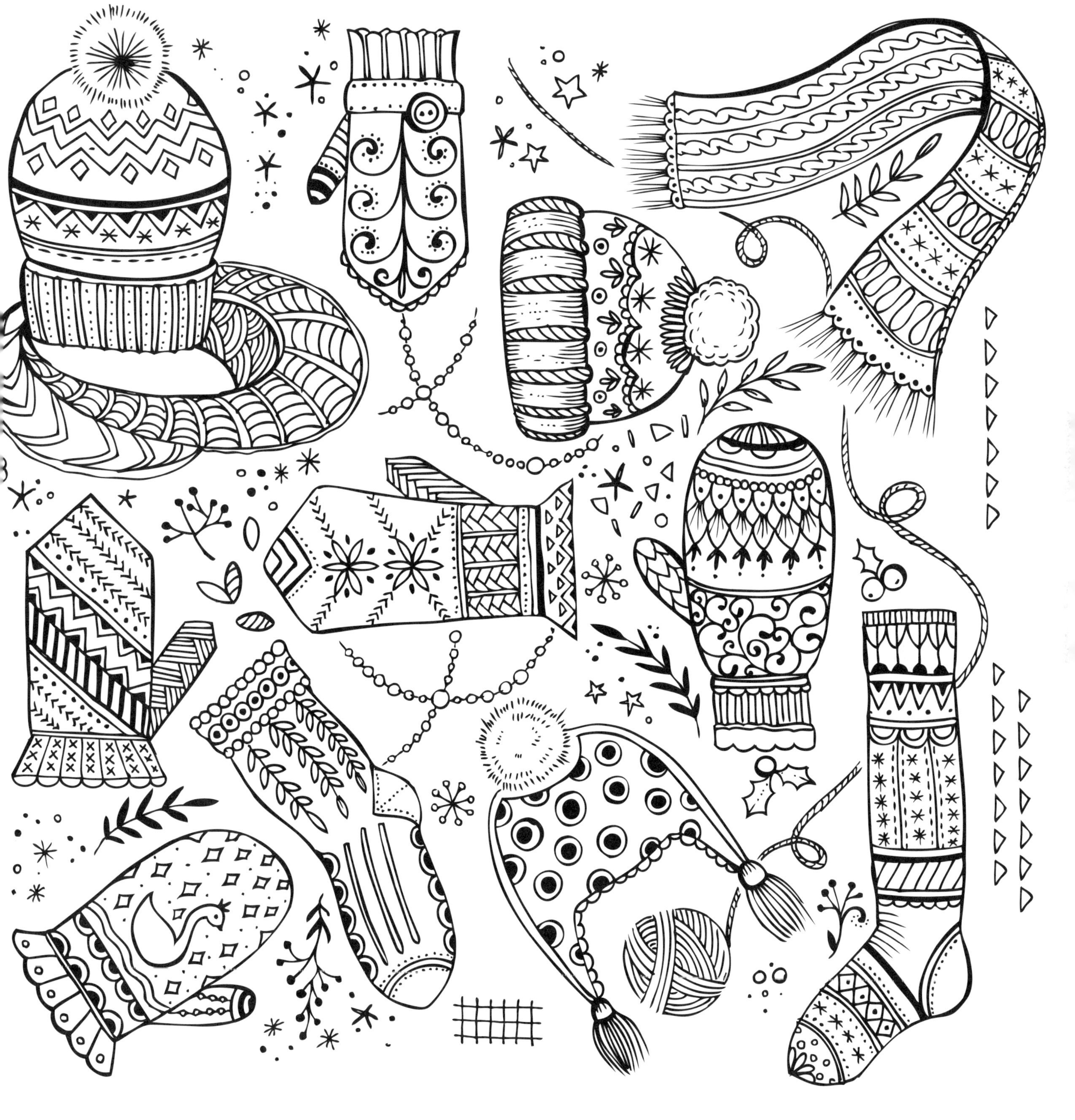

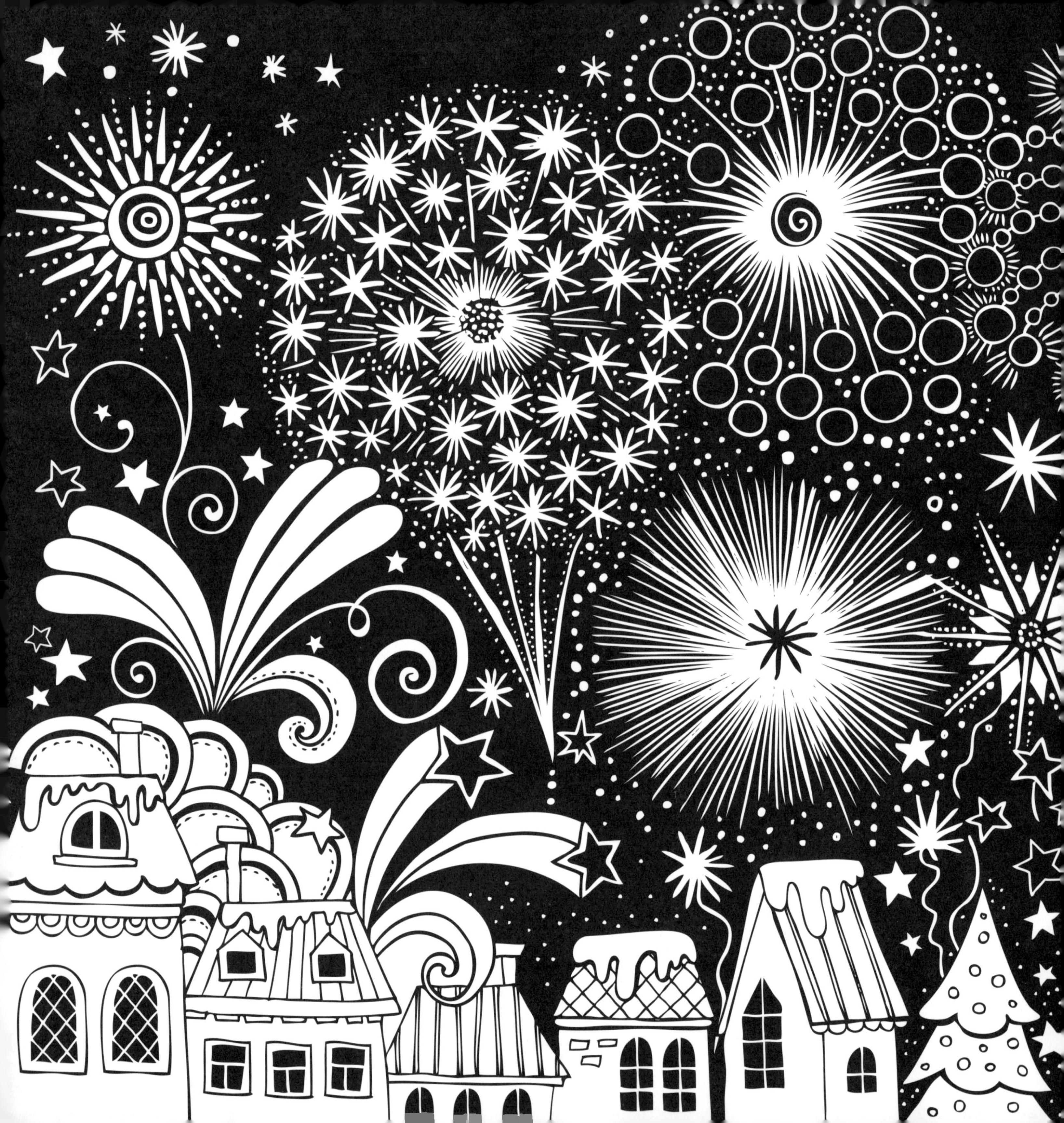

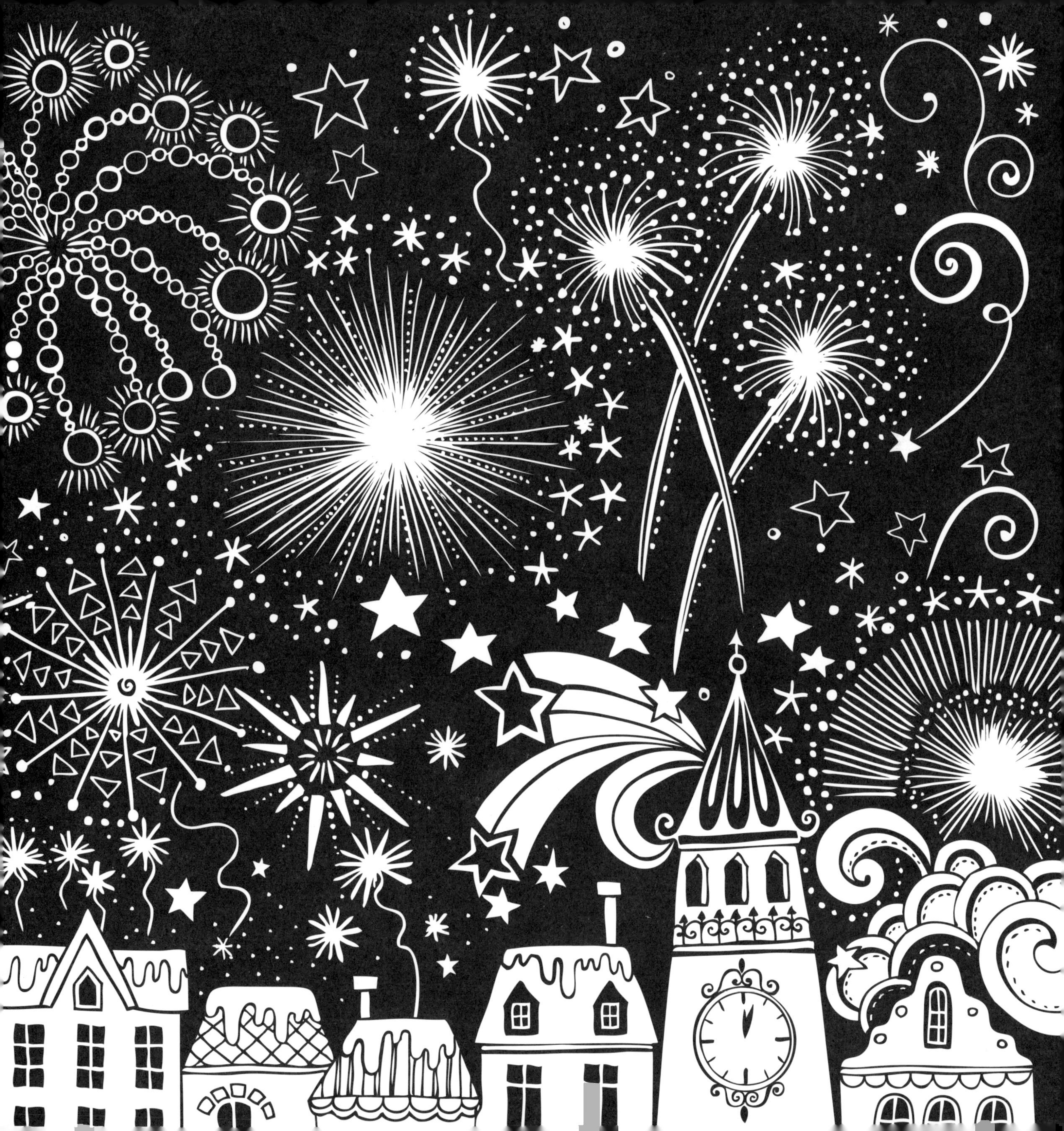

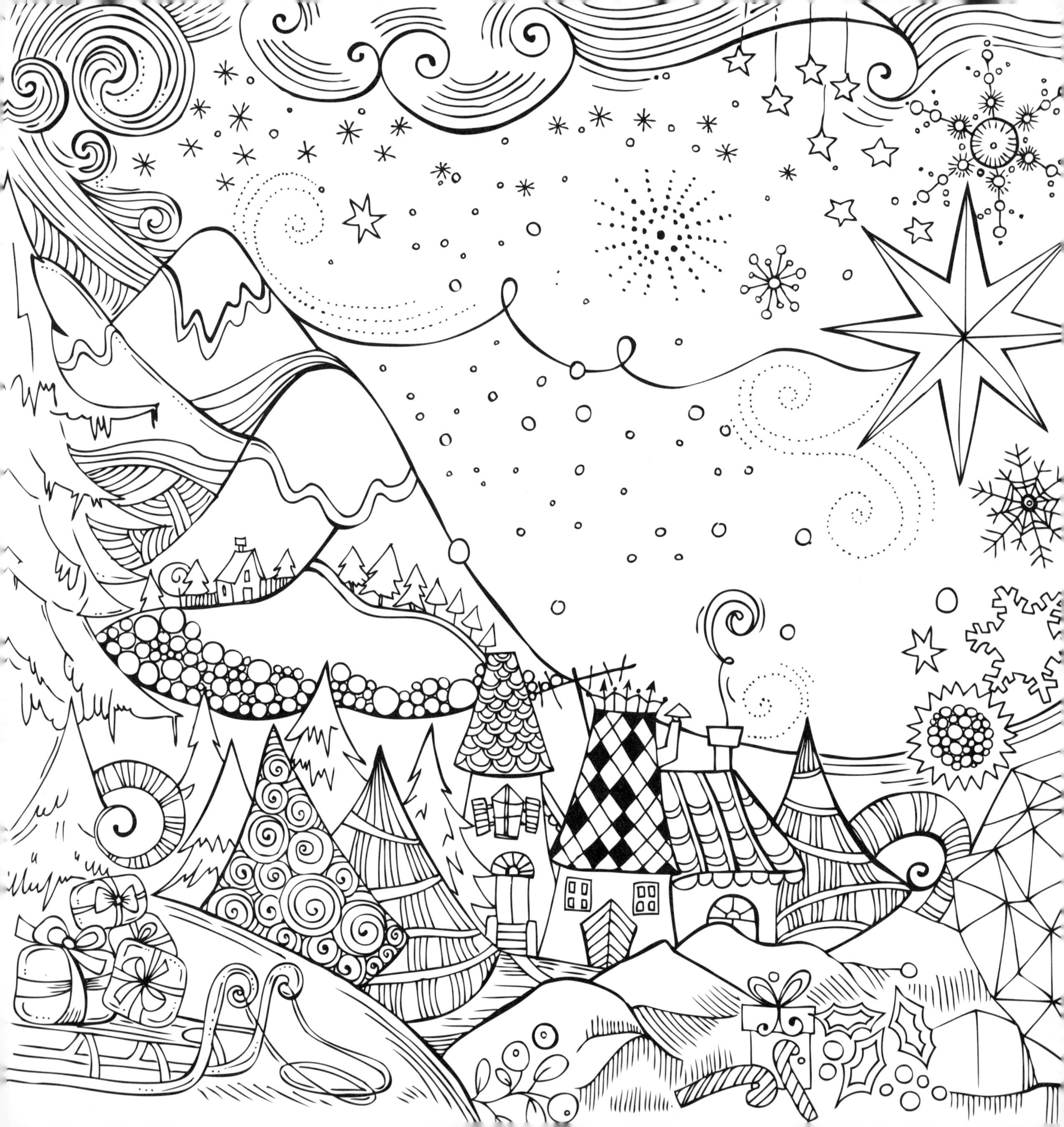

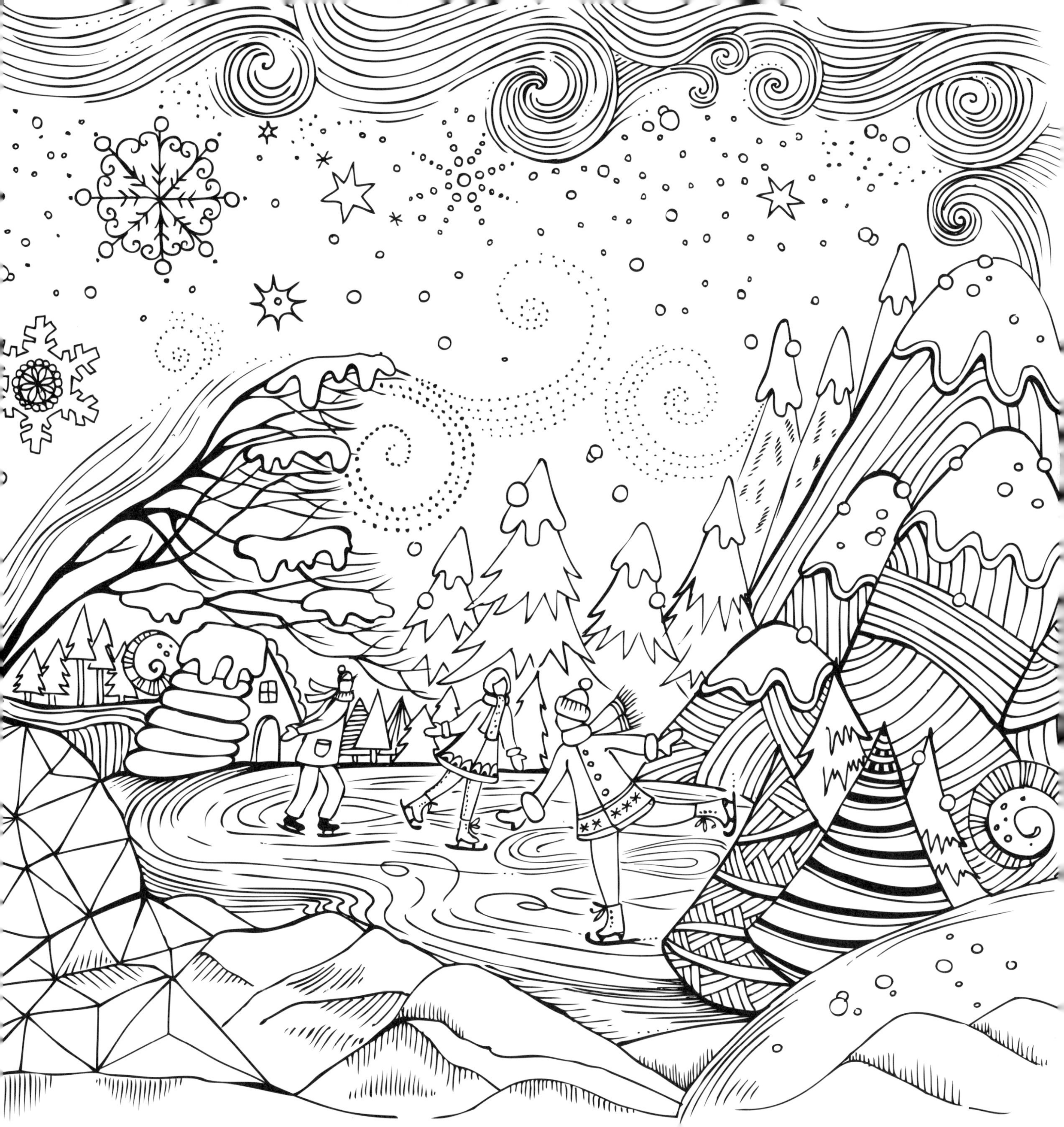

PAPER TEST.

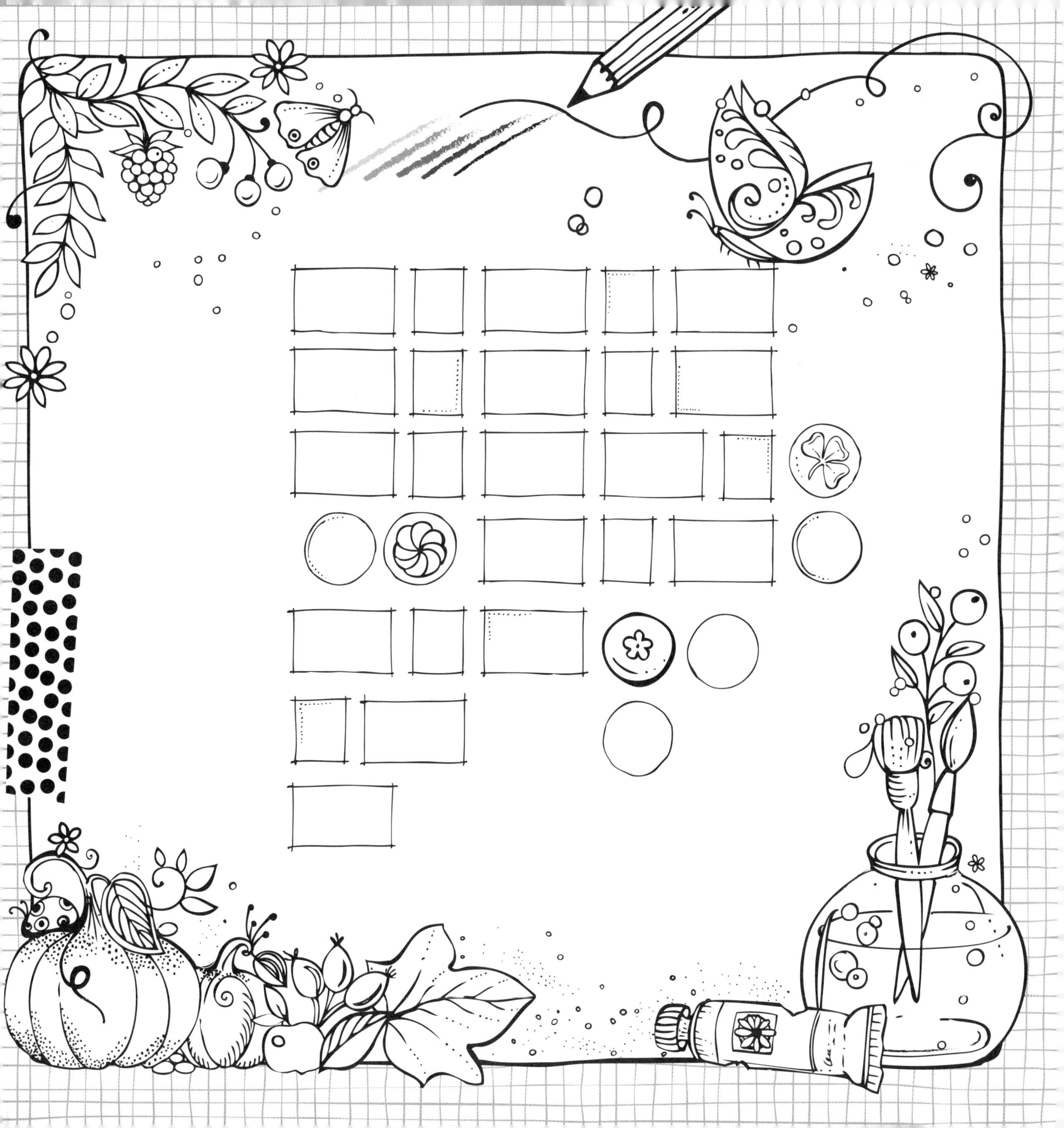

Rita Berman was born in Moldova in 1971 and was passionate about drawing from an early age. She studied architecture and moved to Germany, where she now works as a designer and illustrator. With her unique style, she creates playful works full of endearing details and many of her books are bestsellers. On Instagram, she shares coloring tips and exciting looks behind the scenes via her account @rita.berman. She lives with her family in Frankfurt am Main, Germany.